Introduction

Greetings, culinary adventurers and welcome to a revolution in your kitchen that's set to redefine the way you think about home-cooked meals. "The Ultimate Ninja Dual Zone Air Fryer Cookbook for Beginners" is not merely a collection of recipes; it's your passport to a world where cooking is faster, healthier, and more ingenious than ever before, tailored specifically for the British palate.

In the bustling life of the UK, where time is precious and health is paramount, the Ninja Dual Zone Air Fryer emerges as a beacon of culinary innovation. Whether you're juggling the demands of work and family or simply seeking to infuse a dash of convenience into your meal preparation, this cookbook is crafted with the intention of bringing the art of Ninja Foodi right into the heart of your home.

With over 186 tasty and delightful recipes, this book is designed to escort you, step by step, through the versatile capabilities of your air fryer. Embrace the opportunity to master the art of Ninja Foodi, where efficiency meets ingenuity, without compromising on the flavours we all cherish and love. This book is a celebration of British cuisine, reimagined through the lens of modern cooking technology. It promises not just meals, but experiences; not just satisfaction, but delight.

Moreover, each recipe in "The Ultimate Ninja Dual Zone Air Fryer Cookbook for Beginners" champions the principle of healthy eating. By harnessing the power of air frying, you can indulge in your favourite dishes, knowing you're making choices that are good for your body without sacrificing the joy of eating well.

Your adventure starts now. Happy frying!

ABOUT NINJA DUAL ZONE AIR FRYER

The Ninja Dual Zone Air Fryer is a revolutionary kitchen appliance that lets you cook two different meals at the same time, each at its own perfect temperature. Whether you're feeding a family with picky eaters or simply want to cook up a side dish alongside your main course, the Dual Zone Air Fryer has you covered.

With its two independent cooking zones, you can fry up crispy fries in one zone while roasting vegetables in the other, all without having to sacrifice flavor or quality. And you can enjoy your favorite fried foods with up to 75% less fat than traditional frying methods.

But the Dual Zone Air Fryer is more than just a fryer. It can also dehydrate fruits, vegetables, and even meat for healthy and delicious snacks. And with its air roasting and baking functions, you can roast everything from potatoes to whole chickens for perfectly cooked meals.

So ditch the greasy takeout and unhealthy snacks, and bring home the Ninja Dual Zone Air Fryer. It's the versatile kitchen appliance that lets you cook healthy and delicious meals for the whole family, all at the same time.

> **This publication is produced in black and white, eschewing images, to both reduce the selling price for our customers and lessen the environmental impact associated with the use of color inks. We recognize that some readers may have a preference for color in their books, and we ask for your understanding on this choice. Our aim is to garner your support for future, more premium offerings. We are truly grateful for your understanding and thank you sincerely.**

NINJA DUAL ZONE'S DIFFERENT

6 COOKING FEATURES

1. Dual independent cooking zones: This is the star feature. Cook two different meals at the same time with individual controls for temperature and time.

2. Smart Finish technology: Ensures both zones finish cooking simultaneously, eliminating the wait for one dish to catch up.

3. Air Fry & Max Crisp: Enjoy crispy, golden fried textures with minimal oil using dedicated Air Fry and Max Crisp functions.

4. Roast & Bake: Roast vegetables, meats, and even bake delicious treats with dedicated settings.

5. Reheat & Dehydrate: Reheat leftovers without drying them out and dehydrate fruits and vegetables for healthy snacks.

6. 7.6L capacity: Each basket holds 3.8L, perfect for family meals or cooking larger portions.

7. Fast cooking: Claims up to 75% faster cooking than traditional ovens.

8. Easy cleaning: Dishwasher-safe parts for convenient cleanup.

9. Additional features: Some models include a digital touch screen, built-in thermometer. Recipe inspiration guide.

- **Air Fry**: Enjoy healthier versions of your favorite fried foods like wings, fries, and onion rings with up to 75% less fat.
- **Roast**: Get juicy and evenly cooked roasts for meats, poultry, and even vegetables, thanks to the DualZone's ability to handle different temperatures.
- **Max Crisp**: Elevate your fried food game with this high-powered setting that delivers ultimate crispness.
- **Bake**: Satisfy your sweet and savory cravings with baked goods like cookies, cakes, pizzas, and casseroles.
- **Dehydrate**: Create healthy and flavorful dried fruits, vegetables, and homemade snacks without a dedicated dehydrator.
- **Reheat**: Leftovers get a new lease on life with quick and even reheating that avoids drying them out.

IMPORTANT SAFEGUARDS

- Keep the appliance and cord away from children. It is not for child use.
- Do not place objects on the appliance during operation.
- Avoid placing the appliance near heat sources or inside an oven.
- Never power it from below-counter outlets or through external timers or remote systems.
- Do not use extension cords to mitigate tripping or entanglement risks.
- Do not immerse the appliance or its components in liquids to prevent electric shock.
- Inspect the appliance and cord regularly. Contact Customer Service if any damage or malfunction is noticed.
- Ensure the appliance is assembled correctly before use.
- Do not block air vents during operation to avoid overheating.
- Ensure the appliance and drawer are clean and dry before use.
- This appliance is strictly for indoor household use.
- Place the appliance on a stable, level, clean, and dry surface. Do not move it while in use.
- Keep the appliance away from the edges of countertops.
- Use only accessories recommended by SharkNinja to prevent risk of fire or shock.
- Make sure the drawer is closed before starting the appliance.
- Allow adequate ventilation around the appliance during use.
- Do not operate without the drawer in place.
- Avoid using the appliance for deep-frying.
- The drawer and plate get hot; handle them carefully and place on a heat-resistant surface after use. Avoid contact during or right after cooking.

Table Of Contents

01 — Classic UK Dishes P01-P08

02 — Breakfasts P09-P20

03 — Lunch P21-P35

04 — Dinner/Supper P36-P51

05 — Snacks P52-P60

06 — Sunday and holiday P61-P69

07 — Desserts P70-P82

08 — Vegetarian P83-P92

Classic UK Dishes

- Apple Crumble 1
- Bakewell Tart 1
- Bangers and Mash 2
- Beef Wellington Bites 2
- Black Pudding Scotch Eggs 3
- Bubble and Squeak 4
- Cottage Pie 4
- Fish and Chips 5
- Gammon Steak with Pineapple 5
- Lamb Shank 6
- Shepherd's Pie Bites 6
- Spotted Dick 7
- Steak and Ale Pie 7
- Sticky Toffee Pudding Cups 7
- Potted Shrimp Crostini 8
- Victoria Sponge Cake 8

Breakfasts

- Bacon and Cheese Croissant 9
- Bacon and Cheese Muffins 9
- Bacon and Egg Sandwich 10
- Bacon and Tomato Sandwich 10
- Bacon Roll 11
- Bacon and Egg Cups 11
- Breakfast Burrito 12
- Breakfast Quesadilla 12
- Cheese and Ham Croissant 13
- Egg and Bacon Muffins 13
- Eggs Benedict 14
- Eggs Royale 14
- Frittata 15
- Fried Eggs on Toast 15
- Hash Brown Patties 16
- Haddock Fishcakes 16
- Mushroom and Cheese Quiche 17
- Poached Eggs on Toast 17
- Sausage and Egg Sandwich 18
- Scrambled Eggs on Toast 18
- Smashed Avocado on Toast 19
- Spinach and Mushroom Frittata 19
- Spinach and Feta Omelette 20
- Vegetable Omelette 20

Lunch

- Beef and Black Bean Stir Fry 21
- Beef and Tomato Sandwich 21
- Beef and Vegetable Skewers 22
- Beef Salad 22
- Beef Stroganoff with Rice 23
- Caesar Salad with Grilled Chicken 23
- Cheese Platter 24
- Chicken and Bacon Pie 24
- Chicken and Spinach Salad 25
- Chicken Burger 25
- Chicken Katsu Curry 26
- Chicken Pasta 26
- Empanadas 27
- Ham and Cheese Toastie 27
- Halloumi Burger 28
- Halloumi Sticks 28
- Jacket Potatoes 29
- Margherita Pizza 29
- Meatballs 30

- Pizza Pockets — 30
- Pork Sandwich — 31
- Pork Wrap — 31
- Prawn Cocktail Stuffed Avocado — 32
- Roasted Chickpeas — 32
- Savoury Muffins — 33
- Tofu Stir Fry — 33
- Tortilla Chips — 34
- Vegetable Curry with Naan Bread — 34
- Vegetable Fritters — 35
- Vegetable Paella — 35

Dinner/Supper

- Bang Bang Shrimp — 36
- BBQ Pulled Pork — 36
- BBQ Ribs — 37
- BBQ Tilapia — 37
- Baked Potatoes — 38
- Beef and Potato Curry — 38
- Cajun Shrimp — 39
- Cajun Tilapia — 39
- Chicken and Bacon Potato Skins — 40
- Chicken and Mushroom Gnocchi — 40
- Chicken and Vegetable Frittata — 41, 41
- Cornish Pasties
- Garlic Butter Steak — 42
- Hamburgers — 42
- Honey Mustard Salmon — 43
- Kedgeree — 43
- Liver and Onions — 44
- Lamb and Apricot Tagine — 44
- Lamb and Vegetable Stir-Fry — 45
- Mac and Cheese — 45
- Maple Glazed Salmon — 46
- Maple Glazed Tilapia — 46
- Orange Glazed Pork Chops — 47
- Orange Glazed Salmon — 47
- Pasties — 48
- Salmon with Lemon and Herbs — 48
- Scampi and Chips — 49
- Salmon en Croute — 49
- Teriyaki Tilapia — 50
- Tofu Scramble — 50
- Vegetable Quesadillas — 51
- Welsh Rarebit — 51

Snacks

- Apple Chips — 52
- Banana Bread Fritters — 52
- Calamari Rings — 53
- Cheesy Bacon Fries — 53
- Cheesy Nachos — 54
- Chicken Pakoras — 54
- Chips and Curry Sauce — 55
- Chocolate-Coated Nuts — 55
- Crispy Tofu Bites — 56
- Fish Fingers — 56
- Mini Sausage Rolls — 57
- Mozzarella Sticks — 57
- Mushrooms on Toast — 58
- Onion Bhajis — 58
- Potato Skins — 59
- Prawn Cocktail Skewers — 59
- Samosas — 60
- Sweet Potato Fries — 60

Sunday and holiday

- Baked Camembert — 61
- Baked Stuffed Apples — 61
- Braised Red Cabbage — 62
- Cabbage Rolls — 62
- Cauliflower Cheese — 63
- Corned Beef Hash — 63
- Cornish Pasty — 64
- Glazed Carrots — 64
- Grilled Asparagus — 65
- Honey Glazed Ham — 65
- Lemon Tart — 66
- Mashed Potatoes — 66
- Pigs in Blankets — 67
- Ratatouille — 67
- Salmon En Croute — 68
- Scalloped Potatoes — 68
- Stuffing Balls — 69
- Yam Fries — 69

Desserts

- Apple Turnovers — 70
- Bakewell Tart Bites — 70
- Banana Fritters — 71
- Biscotti — 71
- Blackberry Fool — 72
- Blueberry Muffins — 72
- Bread Pudding — 73
- Carrot Cake Cupcakes — 73
- Chocolate Brownies — 74
- Chocolate Chip Cookies — 74
- Chocolate Lava Cake — 75
- Churros — 75
- Cinnamon Rolls — 76
- Lemon Bars — 76
- Lemon Drizzle Cake — 77
- Lemon Meringue Pie — 77
- Mini Fruit Pies — 78
- Mint Aero Tartlets — 78
- Peach Cobbler — 79
- Pear Tart — 79
- Pumpkin Pie — 80
- Raspberry Bakewell Tarts — 80
- Rhubarb Crisp — 81
- Sticky Toffee Pudding — 81
- Stuffed Dates — 82
- Treacle Tart — 82

Vegetarian

- Aubergine Parmesan — 83
- Butternut Squash Fries — 83
- Cauliflower Wings — 84
- Cheesy Garlic Bread — 84
- Corn on the Cob — 85
- Crispy Onion Rings — 85
- Crispy Polenta Fries — 86
- Crispy Tofu — 86
- Falafel — 87
- Garlic Mushrooms — 87
- Halloumi Fries — 88
- Mushroom Wellington — 88
- Stuffed Bell Peppers — 89
- Stuffed Mushrooms — 89
- Stuffed Portobello Mushrooms — 90
- Sweet Potato Hash Browns — 90
- Vegetable Kebabs — 91
- Vegetable Tempura — 91
- Vegetarian Meatballs — 92
- Vegetarian Quesadillas — 92

Apple Crumble

Prep: 15 Min | Cook: 20 Min | Serves: 4

Ingredient:

For the filling:
- 4-5 medium-sized apples, peeled, cored, and sliced
- 50g granulated sugar
- 1 tablespoon lemon juice
- 1/2 teaspoon ground cinnamon

For the crumble topping:
- 100g plain flour
- 50g unsalted butter, cold and cubed
- 50g rolled oats
- 50g light brown sugar
- 1/2 teaspoon ground cinnamon

Instruction:

1. In a large mixing bowl, combine the sliced apples, granulated sugar, lemon juice, and ground cinnamon. Toss until the apples are evenly coated.
2. Transfer the apple mixture to a baking dish that fits in Zone 1 of the air fryer.
3. In a separate mixing bowl, combine the plain flour, cold cubed butter, rolled oats, light brown sugar, and ground cinnamon. Use your fingertips to rub the butter into the dry ingredients until the mixture resembles coarse breadcrumbs.
4. Spread the crumble topping evenly over the apple filling in the baking dish.
5. Place the baking dish in Zone 1 of the air fryer.
6. Select Zone 1 and choose the AIR FRY program. Set the temperature to 180°C. Cook for 25 minutes, or until the apple filling is bubbling and the crumble topping is golden and crisp. Press the START/STOP button to begin cooking.
7. Once the Apple Crumble is cooked, remove it from the air fryer and let it cool slightly before serving.
8. Serve the **Apple Crumble** warm as a comforting dessert, optionally with a scoop of vanilla ice cream or a dollop of custard. Enjoy the delicious taste of this British-inspired dessert!

CHAPTER 01: CLASSIC UK DISHES

Bakewell Tart

Prep: 30 Min | Cook: 30 Min | Serves: 8

Ingredient:

For the pastry:
- 200g plain flour
- 100g unsalted butter, cold and cubed
- 50g icing sugar
- 1 egg yolk
- 1-2 tablespoons cold water

For the filling:
- 200g raspberry jam
- 150g unsalted butter, softened
- 150g caster sugar
- 3 large eggs
- 150g ground almonds
- 1 teaspoon almond extract
- 25g flaked almonds

Instruction:

1. In a large mixing bowl, combine the plain flour, cold cubed butter, and icing sugar. Use your fingertips to rub the butter into the flour until the mixture resembles breadcrumbs.
2. Add the egg yolk and 1 tablespoon of cold water to the mixture. Mix until the dough comes together, adding more water if needed. Shape the dough into a ball, wrap it in plastic wrap, and refrigerate for 15 minutes.
3. Roll out the pastry on a lightly floured surface to fit a 18cm tart tin. Line the tart tin with the pastry, trimming any excess.
4. Spread the raspberry jam evenly over the pastry base.
5. In a separate mixing bowl, cream together the softened butter and caster sugar until light and fluffy. Add the eggs one at a time, beating well after each addition. Stir in the ground almonds and almond extract.
6. Pour the almond mixture over the raspberry jam in the tart tin, spreading it evenly.
7. Place the tart tin in Zone 1 of the air fryer. Select Zone 1 and choose the BAKE program. Set the temperature to 180°C. Cook for 25-30 minutes, or until the tart filling is set and the pastry is golden brown. Press the START/STOP.
8. Once the Bakewell Tart is cooked, let it cool in the tin for a few minutes. Sprinkle the flaked almonds over the top.
9. Serve the **Bakewell Tart** warm or at room temperature, optionally with a dusting of icing sugar.

Bangers and Mash

Prep: 15 Min | Cook: 20 Min | Serves: 4

Ingredient:

- 4 British pork sausages (bangers)
- 1 kg potatoes, peeled and chopped
- 150ml milk
- 50g butter
- 1 onion, sliced
- 2 cloves of garlic, minced
- 2 tbsp olive oil
- 2 tbsp Worcestershire sauce
- Salt and pepper, to taste
- Fresh parsley, chopped (for garnish)

Instruction:

1. In Zone 1, place the sausages. Select Zone 1, choose the AIR FRY program, and set the temperature to 180°C. Set the time to 20 minutes. Press the START/STOP button to begin air frying the sausages. Turn sausages halfway through cooking for even browning.
2. While sausages cook, boil potato chunks until tender. Drain and return to saucepan. Add butter and milk, mash until smooth. Season with salt and pepper, keep warm. Mash the potatoes with a potato masher until smooth and creamy.
3. In Zone 2, place frying pan or skillet. Add vegetable oil and sliced onion. Select Zone 2, choose the AIR FRY program, and set the temperature to 180°C. Set the time to 10 minutes. Press the START/STOP. Stir the onions occasionally during cooking to ensure even browning.
4. In the same frying pan or skillet in Zone 2, sprinkle the flour over the onions and stir well to coat them. Cook for an additional 1-2 minutes to cook out the raw flour taste.
5. Gradually pour in the beef or onion gravy while stirring continuously to avoid lumps. Cook until the gravy thickens to your desired consistency. Keep the gravy warm.
6. Serve the cooked sausages on a bed of creamy mashed potatoes. Pour the onion gravy over the **sausages and mashed** potatoes. Garnish with chopped fresh parsley, if desired.

CHAPTER 01: CLASSIC UK DISHES

Beef Wellington Bites

Prep: 20 Min | Cook: 20 Min | Serves: 4

Ingredient:

- 400g beef fillet steak
- 200g puff pastry
- 100g pâté (such as liver pâté)
- 1 egg, beaten
- Salt and pepper, to taste
- 1 tablespoon olive oil
- Fresh parsley, for garnish

Instruction:

1. Season the beef fillet steak with salt and pepper. Heat the olive oil in a pan over high heat. Sear the steak on all sides until browned. Remove from heat and let it cool.
2. Roll out the puff pastry on a lightly floured surface to a thickness of about 3mm. Cut the puff pastry into 4 equal squares.
3. Spread a thin layer of pâté onto each square of puff pastry.
4. Place the seared beef fillet in the center of each square. Wrap the puff pastry around the beef, sealing the edges by pressing them together.
5. Brush the beaten egg over the pastry-wrapped beef bites to give them a golden color when cooked.
6. Place the beef Wellington bites in Zone 1 of the air fryer. Select Zone 1 and choose the AIR FRY program. Set the temperature to 200°C. Cook for 20 minutes, or until the pastry is puffed and golden brown. Press the START/STOP button to begin cooking.
7. Once cooked, remove the beef Wellington bites from the air fryer and let them cool slightly before serving.
8. Garnish with fresh parsley and serve as a delightful appetizer or main course. Enjoy the British classic flavors of **Beef Wellington in bite-sized** form!

Black Pudding Scotch Eggs

Prep: 20 Min | Cook: 10 Min | Serves: 4

Ingredient:

- 4 large eggs
- 200g black pudding, crumbled
- 300g sausage meat
- Salt and pepper to taste
- Vegetable oil, for frying
- 50g plain flour
- 2 eggs, beaten
- 100g breadcrumbs

▶ Instruction:

1. Boil the four large eggs for 6 to 7 minutes for a slightly soft-boiled egg or 9 to 10 minutes for a fully hard-boiled egg.
2. While the eggs are boiling, mix together the crumbled black pudding, sausage meat, salt, and pepper in a bowl.
3. Peel the boiled eggs and set them aside.
4. Take one portion of the black pudding and sausage mixture, flatten it in your hand, and wrap it around one peeled egg.
5. Roll each black pudding-covered egg in flour, dip it in beaten eggs, and coat it with breadcrumbs.
6. Carefully place the coated scotch eggs into Zone 1, ensuring they are arranged in a single layer.
7. In Zone 1 of the Air Fryer, add enough vegetable oil to submerge the scotch eggs. Select Zone 1, choose the AIR FRY program at 180°C for 10 minutes to fry the scotch eggs.
8. Press the START/STOP button to begin cooking.
9. After 5 minutes, flip the scotch eggs using tongs or a spatula.
10. Serve the **Black Pudding Scotch Eggs** warm as a delicious appetizer or snack.

CHAPTER 01: CLASSIC UK DISHES

Bubble and Squeak

Prep: 15 Min | Cook: 25 Min | Serves: 4

Ingredient:

- 500g potatoes, peeled and diced
- 200g cooked Brussels sprouts, roughly chopped
- 150g cooked cabbage, roughly chopped
- 1 small onion, finely chopped
- 50g butter
- Salt and pepper to taste
- 4 slices of bacon (optional)
- Vegetable oil, for frying

▶ Instruction:

1. In Zone 1 of the Air Fryer, add the diced potatoes.
2. Select Zone 1, choose the AIR FRY program, and set the temperature to 180°C. Set the cooking time to 15 minutes.
3. Press the START/STOP button to begin cooking.
4. While the potatoes and bacon are cooking, heat the butter in a frying pan over medium heat. Add the chopped onion and cook until softened and lightly browned.
5. Once the potatoes have cooked, carefully remove the lid from Zone 1 and transfer the cooked potatoes to a large mixing bowl. Mash the potatoes using a potato masher or fork.
6. Add the cooked Brussels sprouts, cooked cabbage, and sautéed onions to the mashed potatoes. Season with salt and pepper. Mix well.
7. Shape the potato mixture into patties of your desired size.
8. In Zone 1 of the Air Fryer, add a little vegetable oil and place the potato patties. Select Zone 1, choose the AIR FRY program, and set the temperature to 180°C. Set the cooking time to 10 minutes. Press the START/STOP.
9. Once the cooking time is complete, carefully remove the lid from Zone 1. Serve the **Bubble and Squeak** hot, garnished with the chopped bacon.

Cottage Pie

Prep: 20 Min | Cook: 25 Min | Serves: 4

Ingredient:

- 500g lean ground beef
- 1 medium onion, diced
- 2 cloves garlic, minced
- 1 tablespoon Worcestershire sauce
- 1 tablespoon tomato paste
- 1 teaspoon dried oregano
- 1 teaspoon dried thyme
- 2 cups beef broth
- 1 cup frozen peas
- 1 cup frozen corn
- 1 tablespoon cornstarch
- 1 tablespoon water
- 600g potatoes, peeled and cut into 2.5cm cubes
- 1 tablespoon olive oil
- Salt and pepper to taste

➤ Instruction:

1. In a large bowl, combine the ground beef, onion, garlic, Worcestershire sauce, tomato paste, oregano, thyme, salt, and pepper.
2. Place the meatballs in Zone 1. Select Zone 1, choose the AIR FRY program, and set the temperature to 200°C. Set the time to 10 minutes. Press the START/STOP button to begin cooking.
3. After 10 minutes, check the meatballs. They should be browned on all sides. While the meatballs are cooking, prepare the mashed potatoes. Boil the potatoes in salted water until tender, about 15-20 minutes. Drain the water and mash the potatoes with olive oil, salt, and pepper to taste.
4. Once the meatballs are cooked, set them aside.
5. In a medium saucepan, bring the beef broth to a boil. Add the peas, corn, cornstarch, and water. Stir until the sauce thickens.
6. Add the meatballs to the sauce and stir to combine.
7. Pour the meatball mixture into a 2-liter baking dish. Top with the mashed potatoes and spread evenly.
8. Place the baking dish in Zone 1. Select Zone 1, choose the BAKE program, and set the temperature to 200°C. Set the time to 15 minutes. Press the START/STOP. After 15 minutes, check the cottage pie. Remove the **cottage pie** from the air fryer and let it cool for a few minutes before serving.

CHAPTER 01: CLASSIC UK DISHES

Fish and Chips

Prep: 15 Min | Cook: 25 Min | Serves: 4

Ingredient:

- 4 skinless and boneless cod fillets, each about 150g
- 1 cup all-purpose flour
- 1 teaspoon baking powder
- 1/2 teaspoon salt
- 1/4 teaspoon black pepper
- 1 egg
- 1/2 cup milk
- 1 tablespoon vegetable oil
- 500g potatoes, peeled and cut into 2.5cm chips
- 1 tablespoon olive oil
- Salt and pepper to taste

➤ Instruction:

1. In a large bowl, combine the flour, baking powder, salt, and pepper.
2. In a separate bowl, whisk together the egg and milk.
3. Dip the cod fillets into the egg mixture, then coat them in the flour mixture.
4. Place the coated cod fillets in Zone 1. Select Zone 1, choose the AIR FRY program, and set the temperature to 200°C. Set the time to 10 minutes. Press the START/STOP button to begin cooking.
5. After 10 minutes, check the cod fillets. They should be golden brown and cooked through. If not, cook for an additional 2-3 minutes.
6. While the cod fillets are cooking, prepare the chips. Toss the potato chips with the olive oil, salt, and pepper in a large bowl.
7. Place the chips in Zone 2. Select Zone 2, choose the AIR FRY program, and set the temperature to 200°C. Set the time to 15 minutes. Press the START/STOP button to begin cooking.
8. After 15 minutes, check the chips. They should be golden brown and crispy. If not, cook for an additional 5-10 minutes.
9. Remove the **Fish and Chips** from the air fryer and serve immediately with your favorite dipping sauces, such as tartar sauce or ketchup.

Gammon Steak with Pineapple

Prep: 10 Min | Cook: 15 Min | Serves: 2

Ingredient:

- 2 gammon steaks (about 200g each)
- 4 pineapple rings (canned or fresh)
- 2 tablespoons brown sugar
- 1 tablespoon wholegrain mustard
- 1 tablespoon vegetable oil
- Salt and pepper, to taste

Instruction:

1. In a small bowl, mix together the brown sugar and wholegrain mustard to create a glaze.
2. Brush the gammon steaks with vegetable oil and season with salt and pepper on both sides.
3. Place the gammon steaks in Zone 1 of the air fryer basket and arrange the pineapple rings in Zone 2.
4. Select Zone 1, choose the ROAST program, and set the temperature to 200°C for 15 minutes. Select MATCH. Press the START/STOP button to begin cooking.
5. After 7-8 minutes, carefully flip the gammon steaks and brush them with the brown sugar and mustard glaze. Flip the pineapple rings as well.
6. Close the air fryer and continue cooking for the remaining 7-8 minutes.
7. Once the cooking time is complete, remove the gammon steaks and pineapple rings from the air fryer.
8. Let the gammon steaks rest for a couple of minutes before serving to allow the juices to redistribute.
9. Serve the **Gammon Steak with Pineapple** hot, accompanied by your choice of sides such as mashed potatoes or steamed vegetables.

CHAPTER 01: CLASSIC UK DISHES

Lamb Shank

Prep: 10 Min | Cook: 50 Min | Serves: 2

Ingredient:

- 2 lamb shanks (approximately 400g each)
- 2 tablespoons vegetable oil
- 1 onion, finely chopped
- 2 carrots, peeled and chopped
- 2 garlic cloves, minced
- 2 tablespoons tomato paste
- 500ml beef stock
- 1 tablespoon Worcestershire sauce
- 1 tablespoon balsamic vinegar
- 1 teaspoon dried rosemary
- Salt and pepper to taste

Instruction:

1. Season the lamb shanks with salt and pepper on all sides.
2. In a pan or skillet, heat the vegetable oil over medium heat. Add the lamb shanks and brown them on all sides for about 5 minutes. Remove the lamb shanks from the pan and set them aside.
3. In the same pan, add the chopped onion, carrots, and minced garlic. Sauté for 5 minutes until the vegetables are softened. Add the tomato paste, beef stock, Worcestershire sauce, balsamic vinegar, and dried rosemary to the pan. Stir well to combine.
4. Transfer the vegetable mixture to a baking dish that fits inside the Ninja Dual Zone Air Fryer.
5. Place the lamb shanks on top of the vegetable mixture in the baking dish.
6. Put the baking dish with the lamb shanks and vegetable mixture in Zone 1 of the Air Fryer.
7. Select Zone 1, choose the AIR FRY program, and set the temperature to 180°C for 50 minutes. Press the START/STOP button to begin cooking.
8. After 50 minutes of cooking, carefully remove the baking dish with the lamb shanks and vegetable mixture from the Air Fryer.
9. Serve the **Lamb Shanks** with the vegetable mixture and your choice of sides, such as mashed potatoes or roasted vegetables.

Shepherd's Pie Bites

Prep: 20 Min | Cook: 20 Min | Serves: 4

Ingredient:

- 500g minced lamb or beef
- 1 tablespoon vegetable oil
- 1 small onion, finely chopped
- 1 carrot, finely chopped
- 1 tablespoon tomato paste
- 150ml beef or vegetable stock
- 1 tablespoon Worcestershire sauce
- 1 tablespoon chopped fresh rosemary
- Salt and pepper, to taste
- 500g mashed potatoes
- 50g grated cheddar cheese
- 1 celery stalk
- 2 cloves garlic

Instruction:

1. In a large frying pan, heat the vegetable oil over medium heat. Add the minced lamb or beef and cook until browned. Add the onion, carrot, celery, and minced garlic to the pan. Cook for 5 minutes, or until the vegetables have softened.
2. Stir in the tomato paste, beef or vegetable stock, Worcestershire sauce, chopped rosemary, salt, and pepper. Cook for a few more minutes until the mixture thickens slightly.
3. Remove the pan from the heat and let the mixture cool.
4. Roll out the mashed potatoes into small balls or flatten them into discs, depending on your preferred shape for the Shepherd's Pie Bites.
5. Spoon a small amount of the meat mixture onto each mashed potato shape.
6. Sprinkle grated cheddar cheese on top of each Shepherd's Pie Bite.
7. Place the Shepherd's Pie Bites in Zone 1. Select Zone 1 and choose the AIR FRY program, and set the temperature to 180°C. Set the time to 20 minutes. Press the START/STOP.
8. Serve the **Shepherd's Pie Bites** as a delicious and convenient appetizer or snack.

CHAPTER 01: CLASSIC UK DISHES

Spotted Dick

Prep: 15 Min | Cook: 35 Min | Serves: 6-8

Ingredient:

- 125g self-raising flour
- 50g suet
- 50g caster sugar
- 1/2 tsp mixed spice
- 1/4 tsp ground cinnamon
- 1/4 tsp grated nutmeg
- 1/2 tsp baking powder
- 100g raisins
- 1 egg
- 125ml milk

Instruction:

1. In a large bowl, combine the flour, suet, caster sugar, mixed spice, cinnamon, nutmeg, and baking powder.
2. Add the raisins and mix well.
3. In a separate bowl, whisk together the egg and milk.
4. Add the wet ingredients to the dry ingredients and mix until just combined. Do not overmix.
5. Grease a 1-liter pudding basin with butter or cooking spray.
6. Pour the mixture into the prepared basin.
7. Cover the basin with foil, ensuring it is tightly sealed to prevent steam from escaping.
8. Place the basin in Zone 1 of the Ninja Dual Zone Air Fryer, ensuring it is centered.
9. Select Zone 1, choose the BAKE program, and set the temperature to 180°C. Set the time to 30-35 minutes.
10. Press the START/STOP button to begin cooking.
11. After the cooking time is complete, carefully remove the basin from the air fryer and let it cool for a few minutes.
12. Remove the foil and invert the basin onto a serving plate.
13. Serve the **Spotted Dick** warm with custard or cream.

Steak and Ale Pie

Prep: 15 Min | Cook: 35 Min | Serves: 4

Ingredient:

- 500g beef, cut into cubes
- 2 tablespoons all-purpose flour
- 1 tablespoon olive oil
- 1 onion, chopped
- 2 cloves garlic, minced
- 1 carrot, chopped
- 1 celery stalk, chopped
- 1 tablespoon tomato paste
- 250ml ale
- 250ml beef broth
- 1 teaspoon dried thyme
- Salt and pepper, to taste
- 1 sheet puff pastry, thawed
- 1 egg, beaten

➤ Instruction:

1. In a bowl, coat the beef cubes with all-purpose flour. Place the beef cubes in Zone 1.
2. Select Zone 1, choose the AIR FRY program, and set the temperature to 180°C. Set the time to 20 minutes. Press the START/STOP.
3. In a pan, heat the olive oil over medium heat. Add the onion, garlic, carrot, and celery, and cook until softened.
4. Stir in the tomato paste, ale, beef broth, thyme, salt, and pepper. Bring to a simmer and cook for 10 minutes.
5. Add the cooked beef cubes to the pan and stir to combine.
6. Divide the mixture into 4 individual pie dishes.
7. Roll out the puff pastry on a lightly floured surface and cut out 4 circles slightly larger than the pie dishes.
8. Place the puff pastry circles over the pie dishes, pressing the edges to seal. Brush the tops of the pies with the beaten egg.
9. Evenly dividing pies between the two zones. Select Zone 1, choose the AIR FRY program, and set the temperature to 180°C. Set the time to 15 minutes. Select MATCH. Press the START/STOP.
10. Once cooked, remove the pies from the air fryer and let them cool for a few minutes. Serve and enjoy your **Steak and Ale Pies**!

CHAPTER 01: CLASSIC UK DISHES

Sticky Toffee Pudding Cups

Prep: 20 Min | Cook: 20 Min | Serves: 4

Ingredient:

For the pudding:
- 200g dates, pitted and chopped
- 200ml boiling water
- 1 teaspoon vanilla extract
- 85g unsalted butter, softened
- 175g light brown sugar
- 2 large eggs
- 175g self-raising flour
- 1 teaspoon baking powder

For the toffee sauce:
- 200g light brown sugar
- 150ml double cream
- 50g unsalted butter

➤ Instruction:

1. In pan, place the chopped dates and pour the boiling water over them. Let them sit for 5 minutes to soften.
2. In a separate bowl, cream together the softened butter and light brown sugar until light and fluffy. Add the eggs one at a time, beating well after each addition. Stir in the vanilla extract.
3. In another bowl, whisk together the self-raising flour and baking powder. Gradually add the flour mixture to the butter and sugar mixture, alternating with the soaked dates and their liquid. Mix until well combined.
4. Grease 4 oven-safe cups or ramekins and divide the pudding batter evenly among them, filling them about three-quarters full.
5. Evenly dividing cups between the two zones. Select Zone 1, choose the BAKE program, and set the temperature to 180°C. Set the time to 20 minutes. Select MATCH. Press the START/STOP.
6. While the pudding cups are cooking, prepare the toffee sauce.
7. In a small saucepan, melt together the light brown sugar, double cream, and unsalted butter. Cook over low heat until the sugar has dissolved and the sauce has thickened slightly, stirring occasionally.
8. Once the pudding cups are cooked, let them cool for a few minutes. Serve the warm **pudding cups** with the toffee sauce poured over the top. Optionally, you can also serve them with a dollop of whipped cream or a scoop of vanilla ice cream.

Potted Shrimp Crostini

Prep: 15 Min | Cook: 10 Min | Serves: 4

Ingredient:

- 200g unsalted butter, softened
- 1/2 teaspoon ground nutmeg
- 1/2 teaspoon ground mace
- 1/2 teaspoon ground white pepper
- 1/2 teaspoon paprika
- 1/2 teaspoon Worcestershire sauce
- 1/2 teaspoon lemon juice
- 200g cooked shrimp, peeled and deveined
- 8 slices of baguette, cut into 1.5cm thick slices
- Fresh dill or parsley, for garnish
- Lemon wedges, for serving

Instruction:

1. In Zone 1 of the air fryer, combine the softened butter, ground nutmeg, ground mace, ground white pepper, paprika, Worcestershire sauce, and lemon juice. Mix well until all the ingredients are thoroughly combined.
2. Add the cooked shrimp to the butter mixture in Zone 1. Stir gently to coat the shrimp in the seasoned butter.
3. Select Zone 1, choose the BAKE program, and set the temperature to 180°C. Set the time to 5 minutes.
4. Press the START/STOP button to begin cooking. Cook the shrimp in the seasoned butter until the butter has melted and the shrimp are heated through.
5. While the shrimp are cooking, place the baguette slices in Zone 2. Select Zone 2, choose the BAKE program, and set the temperature to 180°C. Set the time to 5 minutes. Press the START/STOP. Cook the baguette slices until they are toasted and golden brown.
6. Once the shrimp and baguette slices are cooked, carefully remove them from the air fryer.
7. To assemble the crostini, spread a generous amount of the potted shrimp mixture on each toasted baguette slice.
8. Garnish with fresh dill or parsley.
9. Serve the **Potted Shrimp Crostini** with lemon wedges on the side.

CHAPTER 01: CLASSIC UK DISHES

Victoria Sponge Cake

Prep: 20 Min | Cook: 20 Min | Serves: 8

Ingredient:

For the cake:
- 200g unsalted butter, softened
- 200g caster sugar
- 4 large eggs
- 200g self-raising flour
- 1 teaspoon baking powder
- 1 teaspoon vanilla extract

For the filling:
- 150g strawberry jam
- 150ml double cream
- Fresh strawberries, for garnish (optional)
- Icing sugar, for dusting

Instruction:

1. In bowl, cream together the softened butter and caster sugar until light and fluffy. Add the eggs, one at a time, beating well after each addition.
2. In a separate bowl, sift together the self-raising flour and baking powder. Gradually add the sifted flour mixture to the butter and sugar mixture, folding gently until well combined. Stir in the vanilla extract.
3. Grease two 18cm round cake pans and divide the cake batter evenly between them.
4. Place two cake pans in two zones. Select Zone 1, choose the BAKE program, and set the temperature to 180°C. Set the time to 20 minutes. Select MATCH. Press the START/STOP. Cook the cake layers until they are golden brown and a toothpick inserted into the center comes out clean.
5. While the cake layers are cooking, whip the double cream until it forms soft peaks.
6. Once the cake layers are cooked, let them cool completely on a wire rack. Once the cake layers are cooled, spread strawberry jam on one layer and whipped cream on the other layer. Sandwich the two layers together, jam side down, to form the Victoria Sponge Cake.
7. Optionally, garnish the top of the cake with fresh strawberries and dust with icing sugar. Serve the **Victoria Sponge Cake** in slices.

Bacon and Cheese Croissant

Prep: 10 Min | Cook: 10 Min | Serves: 4

Ingredient:

- 4 croissants, split in half
- 4 slices of bacon, cooked
- 4 slices of cheese (cheddar, mozzarella, or your favorite)
- 1 tablespoon butter, melted

Instruction:

1. Evenly dividing croissant halves between the two zones, ensuring they are arranged in a single layer.
2. Select Zone 1, choose the BAKE program, and set the temperature to 200°C. Set the time to 5 minutes. Select MATCH. Press the START/STOP button to begin cooking.
3. After 5 minutes, check the croissants. They should be golden brown. If not, cook for an additional 2-3 minutes.
4. Remove the croissants from the air fryer and place them on a plate.
5. Top each croissant half with a slice of bacon and a slice of cheese.
6. Place the croissants back in both zones.
7. Select Zone 1, choose the BAKE program, and set the temperature to 200°C. Set the time to 5 minutes. Select MATCH. Press the START/STOP button to begin cooking.
8. After 5 minutes, check the croissants. The cheese should be melted and bubbly. If not, cook for an additional 2-3 minutes.
9. Remove the **croissants** from the air fryer and serve immediately.
10. Fresh herbs, such as parsley, chives, or basil, can add a pop of color and freshness to your dish.

CHAPTER 02: BREAKFASTS

Bacon and Cheese Muffins

Prep: 15 Min | Cook: 15 Min | Serves: 6 muffins

Ingredient:

- 150g plain flour
- 2 teaspoons baking powder
- 1/2 teaspoon salt
- 1/4 teaspoon black pepper
- 75g cheddar cheese, grated
- 75g cooked bacon, chopped
- 2 tablespoons fresh chives, chopped
- 1 large egg
- 150ml whole milk
- 2 tablespoons vegetable oil

Instruction:

1. In a mixing bowl, combine the plain flour, baking powder, salt, and black pepper.
2. Add the grated cheddar cheese, chopped bacon, and fresh chives to the dry ingredients. Mix well.
3. In a separate bowl, whisk together the egg, whole milk, and vegetable oil.
4. Pour the wet ingredients into the dry ingredients. Stir until just combined. Be careful not to overmix; a few lumps are fine.
5. Line the muffin cups with paper liners or grease them with a little oil or cooking spray.
6. Divide the batter equally among the muffin cups, filling each about 2/3 full.
7. Place the muffin tray in Zone 1 of the air fryer.
8. Select Zone 1, choose the BAKE program, and set the temperature to 180°C. Set the time to 15 minutes.
9. Press the START/STOP button to begin cooking. Bake the muffins until they are golden brown and a toothpick inserted into the center comes out clean.
10. Once cooked, carefully remove the muffins from the air fryer and let them cool slightly.
11. Serve the **Bacon and Cheese Muffins** warm.

Bacon and Egg Sandwich

Prep: 5 Min | Cook: 15 Min | Serves: 2 sandwich

Ingredient:

- 8 rashers of back bacon
- 4 large eggs
- 4 slices of bread
- 2 tbsp butter
- Salt and pepper, to taste
- Ketchup or brown sauce (optional)

▶ Instruction:

1. In Zone 1 of the Ninja Dual Zone Air Fryer, place the bacon rashers.
2. In Zone 2, place the slices of bread.
3. Select Zone 1, choose the AIR FRY program, and set the temperature to 180°C. Set the time to 10 minutes.
4. Select MATCH to duplicate settings across both zones. Press the START/STOP button to begin cooking.
5. While the bacon and bread are cooking, crack the eggs into a bowl and whisk them lightly. Season with salt and pepper.
6. After 5 minutes of air frying, carefully remove the bread slices from the air fryer and spread butter on one side of each slice.
7. Return the buttered bread slices to Zone 2 of the air fryer and continue air frying for another 5 minutes.
8. In a separate skillet, cook the whisked eggs over medium heat, stirring constantly, until they reach your desired consistency.
9. Once the bacon is crispy and the bread slices are toasted, remove them from the air fryer.
10. Place 2 bacon rashers on each slice of bread.
11. Divide the scrambled eggs evenly between the sandwiches, placing them on top of the bacon.
12. Optionally, add ketchup or brown sauce to taste.
13. Close the **sandwiches** and serve hot.

CHAPTER 02: BREAKFASTS

Bacon and Tomato Sandwich

Prep: 15 Min | Cook: 15 Min | Serves: 6 muffins

Ingredient:

- 150g plain flour
- 2 teaspoons baking powder
- 1/2 teaspoon salt
- 1/4 teaspoon black pepper
- 75g cheddar cheese, grated
- 75g cooked bacon, chopped
- 2 tablespoons fresh chives, chopped
- 1 large egg
- 150ml whole milk
- 2 tablespoons vegetable oil

▶ Instruction:

1. In Zone 1 of the Ninja Dual Zone Air Fryer, place the bacon rashers.
2. In Zone 2, place the slices of bread.
3. Select Zone 1, choose the AIR FRY program, and set the temperature to 180°C. Set the time to 10 minutes. Select MATCH to duplicate settings across both zones. Press the START/STOP button to begin air frying the bacon and bread slices.
4. While the bacon and bread are cooking, slice the tomatoes and prepare any optional ingredients such as lettuce leaves and mayonnaise.
5. After 5 minutes of air frying, carefully remove the bread slices from the air fryer and spread butter on one side of each slice.
6. Return the buttered bread slices to Zone 2 of the air fryer and continue air frying for another 5 minutes.
7. Once the bacon is crispy and the bread slices are toasted, remove them from the air fryer.
8. Place 2 bacon rashers on each slice of bread.
9. Add sliced tomatoes on top of the bacon.
10. Optionally, add lettuce leaves and mayonnaise to taste.
11. Season with salt and pepper.
12. Close the sandwiches and enjoy your **Bacon and Tomato Sandwich**!

Bacon Roll

Prep: 10　Min | Cook: 10　Min | Serves: 4

Ingredient:

- 8 slices of back bacon
- 4 bread rolls
- Butter or spread, for spreading
- Optional toppings: ketchup, brown sauce, or your preferred condiments

▶ Instruction:

1. Split the bread rolls in half and spread butter or your preferred spread on the inside of each half.
2. Roll each slice of bacon tightly, starting from one end to the other.
3. Place four rolled bacon slices in Zone 1 of the air fryer basket, and the other four in Zone 2.
4. Select Zone 1 and choose the AIR FRY program. Set the temperature to 200°C. Set the time to 10 minutes. Select MATCH.
5. Press the START/STOP button to begin cooking.
6. After 5 minutes, carefully flip the bacon rolls in both zones using tongs. Close the air fryer and continue cooking for the remaining 5 minutes.
7. Once the cooking time is complete, remove the bacon rolls from the air fryer.
8. Place two bacon rolls in each bread roll, and add any desired toppings such as ketchup or brown sauce.
9. Serve the **Bacon Rolls** hot and enjoy as a delicious breakfast or snack.

CHAPTER 02: BREAKFASTS

Bacon and Egg Cups

Prep: 10　Min | Cook: 15　Min | Serves: 4

Ingredient:

- 8 slices of bacon
- 4 large eggs
- Salt and pepper, to taste
- Optional toppings: grated cheese, chopped herbs (such as chives or parsley)

▶ Instruction:

1. Line Zone 1 muffin cup with 2 slices of bacon, crossing them to create a cup shape.
2. Place the bacon-lined muffin cups in Zone 1 of the air fryer basket.
3. Select Zone 1 and choose the AIR FRY program. Set the temperature to 180°C. Set the time to 5 minutes. Press the START/STOP button to begin cooking.
4. After 5 minutes, carefully remove the bacon cups from the air fryer and carefully pour out any excess grease.
5. Crack one egg into each bacon cup, being careful not to overflow.
6. Season each egg with salt and pepper, and add any desired toppings such as grated cheese or chopped herbs.
7. Place the bacon and egg cups back into Zone 1 of the air fryer basket.
8. Select Zone 1 and choose the AIR FRY program. Set the temperature to 180°C and the time to 10 minutes. Press the START/STOP button to continue cooking.
9. Once the cooking time is complete, carefully remove the bacon and egg cups from the air fryer.
10. Serve the **Bacon and Egg Cups** hot, and enjoy a delicious and protein-packed breakfast.

Breakfast Burrito

Prep: 15 Min | Cook: 5 Min | Serves: 2

Ingredient:

- 4 large eggs
- 100g back bacon, diced
- 1 small onion, diced
- 1 small bell pepper, diced
- 2 tortilla wraps
- 50g grated cheddar cheese
- Salt and pepper, to taste
- Optional toppings: salsa, sour cream, guacamole

Instruction:

1. In a frying pan, cook the diced bacon over medium heat until crispy. Remove the bacon from the pan and set aside.
2. In the same pan, sauté the diced onion and bell pepper until they become tender and slightly caramelized. Set aside.
3. In a bowl, whisk the eggs and season with salt and pepper.
4. Warm the tortilla wraps according to the package instructions.
5. In the same pan used to cook the bacon, scramble the whisked eggs over medium heat until cooked to your desired consistency.
6. Divide the scrambled eggs, cooked bacon, sautéed onion, and bell pepper between the tortilla wraps. Sprinkle grated cheddar cheese on top.
7. Roll up the tortilla wraps, tucking in the sides to create a burrito.
8. Place the burritos in Zone 1 of the air fryer basket.
9. Select Zone 1 and choose the AIR FRY program. Set the temperature to 180°C and the time to 5 minutes. Press the START/STOP button to continue cooking.
10. Once the cooking time is complete, carefully remove the breakfast burritos from the air fryer.
11. Serve the **Breakfast Burritos** hot, and add optional toppings such as salsa, sour cream, or guacamole.

CHAPTER 02: BREAKFASTS

Breakfast Quesadilla

Prep: 10 Min | Cook: 10 Min | Serves: 2

Ingredient:

- 4 medium-sized flour tortillas
- 100g grated cheddar cheese
- 4 large eggs
- 50g cooked bacon, crumbled
- 1 small onion, diced
- 1 small bell pepper, diced
- Salt and pepper, to taste
- Optional toppings: salsa, sour cream, guacamole

Instruction:

1. In a frying pan, cook the diced bacon over medium heat until crispy. Remove the bacon from the pan and set aside.
2. In the same pan, sauté the diced onion and bell pepper until they become tender and slightly caramelized.
3. In a bowl, combine the cooked bacon, sautéed onion, bell pepper, grated cheddar cheese, chopped parsley, salt, and pepper. Mix well.
4. Place tortillas on Zone 1 and 2 of the air fryer basket.
5. Divide the bacon and vegetable mixture evenly between the tortillas, spreading it over one half of each tortilla.
6. Fold the other half of each tortilla over the filling to create a half-moon shape.
7. Select Zone 1 and choose the AIR FRY program. Set the temperature to 180°C and the time to 5 minutes. Select MATCH. Press the START/STOP button to begin cooking.
8. Once the cooking time is complete, carefully remove the quesadillas from the air fryer.
9. Allow the quesadillas to cool slightly before cutting them into wedges.
10. Serve the **Breakfast Quesadillas** hot, and add optional toppings such as salsa, sour cream, or guacamole.

Cheese and Ham Croissant

Prep: 5 Min | Cook: 8 Min | Serves: 2

Ingredient:

- 2 croissants
- 4 slices of ham
- 100g grated cheddar cheese
- 1 tablespoon Dijon mustard (optional)
- Cooking spray or a small amount of oil

▶ Instruction:

1. Slice the croissants in half lengthwise.
2. If desired, spread a thin layer of Dijon mustard on the bottom half of each croissant.
3. Place 2 slices of ham on each bottom half of the croissants.
4. Sprinkle grated cheddar cheese evenly over the ham.
5. Gently place the top halves of the croissants over the cheese to create sandwiches.
6. Lightly grease the Zone 1 of the air fryer basket with cooking spray or a small amount of oil.
7. Place the croissant sandwiches in Zone 1 of the air fryer basket.
8. Select Zone 1, choose the ROART program. Set the temperature to 180°C and the time to 8 minutes. Press the START/STOP button to begin cooking.
9. Once the cooking time is complete, carefully remove the **Cheese and Ham Croissants** from the air fryer basket.
10. Allow the croissants to cool slightly before serving.

CHAPTER 02: BREAKFASTS

Egg and Bacon Muffins

Prep: 10 Min | Cook: 12 Min | Serves: 4

Ingredient:

- 4 English muffins
- 4 slices of back bacon
- 4 large eggs
- 30g grated cheddar cheese
- Salt and pepper, to taste
- Cooking spray or a small amount of oil

▶ Instruction:

1. Lightly grease the Zone 1 of the air fryer basket with cooking spray or a small amount of oil.
2. Place the bacon slices in Zone 1 of the air fryer basket. Select Zone 1 and choose the AIR FRY program. Set the temperature to 180°C and the time to 8 minutes. Press the START/STOP.
3. Meanwhile, slice the English muffins in half horizontally.
4. In a bowl, whisk the eggs until well beaten. Season with salt and pepper. In a frying pan, pour the beaten eggs and cook for 4 minutes.
5. Once the bacon is cooked, carefully remove it from the air fryer basket and set it aside.
6. Place the English muffins, cut side up, in Zone 1 of the air fryer basket.
7. Select Zone 1 and choose the AIR FRY program. Set the temperature to 180°C for 4 minutes. Press the START/STOP.
8. Once the muffins is cooked, carefully remove them from the air fryer basket.
9. Assemble the Egg and Bacon Muffins by placing one slice of bacon on the bottom half of each English muffin. Top each slice of bacon with a portion of the cooked egg.
10. Sprinkle grated cheddar cheese over the eggs.
11. Place the top halves of the English muffins on top of the cheese to create sandwiches. Serve the **Egg and Bacon Muffins** hot.

Eggs Benedict

Prep: 15 Min | Cook: 15 Min | Serves: 2

Ingredient:

- 2 English muffins
- 4 slices of back bacon
- 4 large eggs
- 2 egg yolks
- 1 tablespoon lemon juice
- 100g unsalted butter, melted
- Salt and pepper, to taste
- Chopped fresh chives, for garnish (optional)

Instruction:

1. Lightly grease Zone 1 of the air fryer basket with cooking spray or a small amount of oil. Place the bacon slices in Zone 1 of the air fryer basket.
2. Select Zone 1 and choose the AIR FRY program. Set the temperature to 180°C for 10 minutes. Press the START/STOP.
3. Meanwhile, slice the English muffins in half horizontally. Set aside.
4. In a bowl, whisk together the egg yolks and lemon juice. Slowly drizzle in the melted butter while whisking continuously to create a hollandaise sauce. Season with salt and pepper. Pour the hollandaise sauce into the pan and cook for 5 minutes.
5. Place the English muffins in Zone 1 of the air fryer basket. Select Zone 1 and choose the AIR FRY program. Set the temperature to 180°C and the time to 5 minutes. Press the START/STOP.
6. While the muffins are toasting, poach the eggs in a separate pot of simmering water until the whites are set but the yolks are still runny, about 3-4 minutes.
7. Assemble the Eggs Benedict by placing one slice of bacon on each toasted English muffin half. Carefully place a poached egg on top of each bacon slice.
8. Drizzle the hollandaise sauce over the poached eggs.
9. Garnish with chopped fresh chives, if desired. Serve the **Eggs Benedict** immediately.

CHAPTER 02: BREAKFASTS

Eggs Royale

Prep: 10 Min | Cook: 15 Min | Serves: 2

Ingredient:

- 2 English muffins
- 4 slices of smoked salmon
- 4 large eggs
- 2 egg yolks
- 1 tablespoon lemon juice
- 100g unsalted butter, melted
- Salt and pepper, to taste
- Chopped fresh dill, for garnish (optional)

Instruction:

1. Lightly grease the Zone 1 of the air fryer basket with cooking spray or a small amount of oil.
2. Place the English muffins, cut side up, in Zone 1 of the air fryer basket.
3. Select Zone 1 and choose the AIR FRY program. Set the temperature to 180°C and the time to 5 minutes. Press the START/STOP button to begin cooking.
4. In a bowl, whisk together the egg yolks and lemon juice until well combined. Slowly drizzle in the melted butter while whisking continuously to create a hollandaise sauce. Season with salt and pepper.
5. Pour the hollandaise sauce into a pan danf cook for 5 minutes.
6. While the muffins are toasting, poach the eggs in a separate pot of simmering water until the whites are set but the yolks are still runny, about 3-4 minutes.
7. Place 2 slices of smoked salmon on each toasted English muffin half.
8. Once the eggs are poached, carefully place one egg on top of each slice of smoked salmon.
9. Drizzle the hollandaise sauce over the poached eggs.
10. Garnish with chopped fresh dill, if desired. Serve the **Eggs Royale** immediately.

Frittata

Prep: 10 Min | Cook: 20 Min | Serves: 4

Ingredient:

- 6 large eggs
- 120ml milk
- 1/2 teaspoon salt
- 1/4 teaspoon black pepper
- 1/2 teaspoon dried herbs (such as thyme, basil, or oregano)
- 1 tablespoon olive oil
- 1 small onion, diced
- 1 bell pepper, diced
- 100g mushrooms, sliced
- 50g grated cheddar cheese
- Fresh herbs (such as parsley or chives) for garnish (optional)

Instruction:

1. In a large bowl, whisk together the eggs, milk, salt, black pepper, and dried herbs until well combined.
2. Lightly grease Zone 1 of the air fryer basket with olive oil.
3. Pour the egg mixture into Zone 1 of the air fryer basket.
4. Add diced onions, bell peppers, and sliced mushrooms on top of the egg mixture in Zone 1.
5. Select Zone 1 and choose the AIR FRY program. Set the temperature to 180°C and the time to 20 minutes.
6. Press the START/STOP button to begin cooking.
7. Once the cooking time is complete, carefully remove the frittata from the air fryer basket.
8. Allow the frittata to cool slightly before slicing into wedges.
9. Garnish with fresh herbs, if desired.
10. Serve the **frittata** warm or at room temperature.

CHAPTER 02: BREAKFASTS

Fried Eggs on Toast

Prep: 5 Min | Cook: 5 Min | Serves: 2

Ingredient:

- 4 slices of bread
- 4 large eggs
- Butter or cooking spray, for greasing
- Salt and pepper, to taste
- Optional toppings: chopped fresh herbs (e.g., chives, parsley), grated cheese, sliced avocado

Instruction:

1. Grease Zone 1 of the air fryer basket with butter or cooking spray.
2. Place the bread slices in Zone 1 of the air fryer basket.
3. Select Zone 1 and the AIR FRY program. Set the temperature to 180°C and the time to 3 minutes. Press the START/STOP button to begin toasting the bread.
4. While the bread is toasting, crack the eggs into a small bowl or ramekins. Season with salt and pepper.
5. After 3 minutes, open the air fryer and carefully flip the bread slices. Make space for the eggs by pushing the bread slices to one side.
6. In a frying pan, melt butter or cooking spray.
7. Gently pour the cracked eggs, being careful not to break the yolks and cook for another 2 minutes or until the eggs are cooked to your desired level of doneness (e.g., runny yolk or fully cooked).
8. Serve the fried eggs on top of the toasted bread slices. Season with additional salt and pepper, if desired.
9. Optional: Add **Fried Eggs on Toast** with your preferred toppings such as chopped fresh herbs, grated cheese, or sliced avocado.

Hash Brown Patties

Prep: 10 Min | Cook: 15 Min | Serves: 4

Ingredient:

- 4 medium-sized potatoes
- 1 small onion, grated
- 2 tablespoons all-purpose flour
- 1 teaspoon salt
- 1/2 teaspoon black pepper
- Cooking spray or vegetable oil, for greasing

Instruction:

1. Peel the potatoes and rinse them under cold water. Grate the potatoes using a box grater or a food processor.
2. Place the grated potatoes in a clean kitchen towel and squeeze out any excess moisture.
3. In a large bowl, combine the grated potatoes, grated onion, flour, salt, and black pepper. Mix well.
4. Take a portion of the potato mixture and shape it into a flat patty, about 2cm thick. Repeat with the remaining mixture to make additional patties.
5. Lightly grease Zone 1 of the air fryer basket with cooking spray or vegetable oil. Place the hash brown patties in both zones of the air fryer basket, ensuring they are arranged in a single layer.
6. Select Zone 1 and choose the AIR FRY program. Set the temperature to 200°C and the time to 15 minutes.
7. Press the START/STOP button to begin cooking.
8. After 15 minutes, carefully remove the air fryer basket and check the hash brown patties. They should be golden brown and crispy.
9. Once cooked to your liking, remove the **Hash Brown Patties** from the air fryer and serve them hot as a delightful breakfast side dish.

CHAPTER 02: BREAKFASTS

Haddock Fishcakes

Prep: 20 Min | Cook: 15 Min | Serves: 4

Ingredient:

- 300g haddock fillets, cooked and flaked
- 400g potatoes, peeled, boiled, and mashed
- 1 small onion, finely chopped
- 2 tablespoons fresh parsley, chopped
- 1 tablespoon lemon juice
- 1 teaspoon Dijon mustard
- Salt and pepper, to taste
- Flour, for coating
- 1 large egg, beaten
- Breadcrumbs, for coating
- Cooking spray or vegetable oil, for greasing

Instruction:

1. In a large bowl, combine the flaked haddock, mashed potatoes, chopped onion, fresh parsley, lemon juice, Dijon mustard, salt, and pepper. Mix well until all the ingredients are evenly incorporated.
2. Take a portion of the fishcake mixture and shape it into a patty, about 2cm thick. Repeat with the remaining mixture to make additional fishcakes.
3. Lightly coat each fishcake with flour, then dip it into the beaten egg, and finally coat it with breadcrumbs, pressing gently to adhere.
4. Lightly grease Zone 1 of the air fryer basket with cooking spray or a small amount of oil.
5. Place the fishcakes in Zone 1 of the air fryer basket, ensuring they are arranged in a single layer.
6. Select Zone 1 and choose the AIR FRY program. Set the temperature to 200°C and the time to 15 minutes.
7. Press the START/STOP button to begin cooking.
8. After 15 minutes, carefully remove the air fryer basket and check if the fishcakes are golden brown and crispy.
9. Once cooked to your liking, remove the **Haddock Fishcakes** from the air fryer basket, and serve them hot as a delicious English breakfast dish.

Mushroom and Cheese Quiche

Prep: 15 Min | Cook: 25 Min | Serves: 4-6

Ingredient:

- 1 ready-made shortcrust pastry crust (about 230g)
- 200g mushrooms, sliced
- 1 small onion, finely chopped
- 150g cheddar cheese, grated
- 4 large eggs
- 200ml milk
- 1 teaspoon dried thyme
- Salt and pepper, to taste
- Fresh parsley, chopped (for garnish)

Instruction:

1. Lightly grease Zone 1 of the air fryer basket with cooking spray or a small amount of oil.
2. Roll out the shortcrust pastry and line Zone 1 of the air fryer basket with the pastry crust, pressing it gently against the sides.
3. In a frying pan, sauté the sliced mushrooms and chopped onion until they are cooked and any excess moisture has evaporated. Set aside.
4. In a bowl, whisk together the eggs, milk, dried thyme, salt, and pepper.
5. Sprinkle half of the grated cheddar cheese over the pastry crust in Zone 1. Spread the sautéed mushrooms and onions evenly over the cheese.
6. Pour the egg mixture over the mushrooms and onions in the air fryer basket and place it in Zone 1.
7. Sprinkle the remaining grated cheddar cheese on top.
8. Select Zone 1 and choose the AIR FRY program. Set the temperature to 180°C for 25 minutes. Press the START/STOP.
9. After 25 minutes, carefully remove the air fryer basket and check if the quiche is set and golden brown on top.
10. Allow the **Mushroom and Cheese Quiche** to cool slightly before serving. Garnish with freshly chopped parsley.

CHAPTER 02: BREAKFASTS

Poached Eggs on Toast

Prep: 5 Min | Cook: 7 Min | Serves: 2

Ingredient:

- 4 slices of bread (white or wholemeal)
- 4 large eggs
- 2 teaspoons white vinegar
- Salt and pepper, to taste
- Butter, for spreading
- Fresh chives or parsley, chopped (for garnish)

Instruction:

1. Lightly grease Zone 1 of the air fryer basket with cooking spray or a small amount of oil.
2. Place the bread slices in Zone 1 of the air fryer basket.
3. Select Zone 1 and choose the AIR FRY program. Set the temperature to 180°C and the time to 5 minutes.
4. Press the START/STOP button to begin toasting the bread.
5. While the bread is toasting, fill a small saucepan with water and bring it to a gentle simmer over medium heat.
6. Add the white vinegar to the simmering water. Crack one egg into a small bowl or ramekin, taking care not to break the yolk.
7. Create a gentle whirlpool in the simmering water using a spoon.
8. Carefully slide the egg into the center of the whirlpool. Allow it to cook for about 3-4 minutes for a soft poached egg or longer if desired.
9. Use a slotted spoon to carefully remove the poached egg from the water and place it on a plate lined with kitchen paper to drain excess water.
10. Once the bread is toasted, remove the air fryer basket and spread butter on the bread slices. Season with salt and pepper.
11. Place a **poached egg** on each slice of toast. Garnish with freshly chopped chives or parsley.

Sausage and Egg Sandwich

Prep: 10 Min | Cook: 18 Min | Serves: 2

Ingredient:

- 4 pork sausages
- 4 slices of bread (white or wholemeal)
- 4 large eggs
- 1 tablespoon butter
- Salt and pepper, to taste
- Tomato ketchup or brown sauce (optional)

▶ Instruction:

1. Lightly grease Zone 1 of the air fryer basket with cooking spray or a small amount of oil.
2. Place the sausages in Zone 1 of the air fryer basket.
3. Select Zone 1 and choose the AIR FRY program. Set the temperature to 180°C for 15 minutes. Press the START/STOP.
4. While the sausages are cooking, crack the eggs into a small bowl or ramekin. Lightly beat them with a fork and season with salt and pepper.
5. In a frying pan, melt the butter over medium heat. Pour the beaten eggs into the pan and cook, stirring gently, until they reach your desired consistency. Remove the pan from the heat.
6. Once the sausages are cooked, remove them from the air fryer basket and set them aside.
7. Place the bread slices in Zone 1 of the air fryer basket.
8. Select Zone 1 and choose the AIR FRY program. Set the temperature to 180°C for 3 minutes. Press the START/STOP.
9. While the bread is toasting, slice the cooked sausages lengthwise.
10. Once the bread is toasted, assemble the sandwich by placing two sausage halves on one slice of bread. Spoon the scrambled eggs on top of the sausages. Top with the remaining slice of bread.
11. Serve the **sausage and egg sandwich** hot with tomato ketchup or brown sauce, if desire

---

CHAPTER 02: BREAKFASTS

Scrambled Eggs on Toast

Prep: 5 Min | Cook: 5 Min | Serves: 2

Ingredient:

- 4 slices of bread (white or wholemeal)
- 4 large eggs
- 60ml milk
- 1 tablespoon butter
- Salt and pepper, to taste
- Fresh chives or parsley, chopped (for garnish)

▶ Instruction:

1. Lightly grease Zone 1 of the air fryer basket with cooking spray or a small amount of oil.
2. Place the bread slices in Zone 1 of the air fryer basket.
3. Select Zone 1 and choose the AIR FRY program. Set the temperature to 180°C and the time to 5 minutes.
4. Press the START/STOP button to begin toasting the bread.
5. While the bread is toasting, crack the eggs into a bowl. Add the milk and season with salt and pepper. Whisk together until well combined.
6. In a frying pan, melt the butter over medium heat.
7. Pour the egg mixture into the pan and cook, stirring gently, until the eggs are soft and slightly runny.
8. Once the bread is toasted, remove the air fryer basket and spread butter on the bread slices.
9. Spoon the scrambled eggs onto the buttered toast slices.
10. Garnish the **Scrambled Eggs on Toast** with freshly chopped chives or parsley.

Smashed Avocado on Toast

Prep: 5 Min | Cook: 3 Min | Serves: 2

Ingredient:

- 2 ripe avocados
- 1 small lime, juiced
- 1 small garlic clove, minced
- Salt and pepper, to taste
- 4 slices of bread (white or wholemeal)
- Olive oil, for drizzling
- Red chili flakes or fresh herbs (optional, for garnish)

▶ Instruction:

1. Lightly grease Zone 1 of the air fryer basket with cooking spray or a small amount of oil.
2. Place the bread slices in Zone 1 of the air fryer basket.
3. Select Zone 1 and choose the AIR FRY program. Set the temperature to 180°C and the time to 3 minutes.
4. Press the START/STOP button to begin toasting the bread.
5. While the bread is toasting, cut the avocados in half, remove the pits, and scoop the flesh into a bowl.
6. Mash the avocado with a fork until desired consistency is reached.
7. Add the lime juice, minced garlic, salt, and pepper to the mashed avocado. Mix well to combine.
8. Once the bread is toasted, remove the air fryer basket and place the slices on a serving plate.
9. Drizzle the toasted bread slices with olive oil.
10. Spread the smashed avocado mixture evenly on top of the toasted bread slices.
11. Sprinkle with red chili flakes or fresh herbs, if desired, for added flavor and garnish.
12. Your delicious **Smashed Avocado on Toast** is now ready to be enjoyed!

CHAPTER 02: BREAKFASTS

Spinach and Mushroom Frittata

Prep: 10 Min | Cook: 20 Min | Serves: 4

Ingredient:

- 6 large eggs
- 100g fresh spinach, roughly chopped
- 100g mushrooms, sliced
- 1 small onion, finely chopped
- 50g cheddar cheese, grated
- 2 tablespoons olive oil
- Salt and pepper, to taste

▶ Instruction:

1. In a frying pan, heat 1 tablespoon of olive oil over medium heat.
2. Add the chopped onion and sliced mushrooms to the pan. Sauté until the mushrooms are cooked and the onions are translucent.
3. Add the chopped spinach to the pan and cook until wilted. Remove the pan from heat and set aside.
4. In a bowl, whisk the eggs together until well beaten. Season with salt and pepper.
5. Pour the cooked vegetables into the beaten eggs and mix well.
6. Lightly grease Zone 1 of the air fryer basket with cooking spray or a small amount of oil.
7. Pour the egg and vegetable mixture into Zone 1 of the air fryer basket.
8. Select Zone 1 and choose the AIR FRY program. Set the temperature to 180°C and the time to 20 minutes.
9. Press the START/STOP button to begin cooking the frittata.
10. After 20 minutes, carefully remove the frittata from the air fryer basket and sprinkle grated cheddar cheese on top.
11. Return the frittata to the air fryer basket and cook for an additional 2 minutes to melt the cheese.
12. Once cooked, remove the frittata from the air fryer and let it cool slightly.
13. Cut the **Spinach and Mushroom Frittata** into wedges and serve warm.

Spinach and Feta Omelette

Prep: 10 Min | Cook: 10 Min | Serves: 2

Ingredient:

- 4 large eggs
- 100g fresh spinach, roughly chopped
- 50g feta cheese, crumbled
- 1 small onion, finely chopped
- 1 tablespoon olive oil
- Salt and pepper, to taste

Instruction:

1. In a frying pan, heat the olive oil over medium heat.
2. Add the chopped onion to the pan and sauté until it becomes translucent.
3. Add the chopped spinach to the pan and cook until wilted. Remove the pan from heat and set it aside.
4. In a bowl, whisk the eggs together until well beaten. Season with salt and pepper.
5. Pour the cooked spinach and onion mixture into the beaten eggs and mix well.
6. Lightly grease Zone 1 of the air fryer basket with cooking spray or a small amount of oil. Pour the egg and vegetable mixture into Zone 1 of the air fryer basket.
7. Select Zone 1 and choose the AIR FRY program. Set the temperature to 180°C and the time to 10 minutes. Press the START/STOP button to begin cooking the omelette.
8. After 10 minutes, carefully remove the omelette from the air fryer basket and sprinkle the crumbled feta cheese on top.
9. Return the omelette to the air fryer basket and cook for an additional 1-2 minutes to melt the cheese.
10. Once cooked, remove the omelette from the air fryer and let it cool slightly. Cut the **Spinach and Feta Omelette** into wedges and serve warm.

CHAPTER 02: BREAKFASTS

Vegetable Omelette

Prep: 10 Min | Cook: 10 Min | Serves: 2

Ingredient:

- 4 large eggs
- 1 small onion, finely chopped
- 1 small bell pepper, diced
- 100g mushrooms, sliced
- 50g baby spinach leaves
- 50g grated cheddar cheese
- 1 tablespoon olive oil
- Salt and pepper, to taste

Instruction:

1. In a frying pan, heat the olive oil over medium heat.
2. Add the chopped onion to the pan and sauté until it becomes translucent.
3. Add the diced bell pepper and sliced mushrooms to the pan. Cook until the vegetables are tender. Remove the pan from heat and set it aside.
4. In a bowl, whisk the eggs together until well beaten. Season with salt and pepper.
5. Pour the cooked vegetables into the beaten eggs and mix well.
6. Lightly grease Zone 1 of the air fryer basket with cooking spray or a small amount of oil.
7. Pour the egg and vegetable mixture into Zone 1 of the air fryer basket.
8. Select Zone 1 and choose the AIR FRY program. Set the temperature to 180°C and the time to 10 minutes.
9. Press the START/STOP button to begin cooking the omelette.
10. After 10 minutes, carefully remove the omelette from the air fryer basket and sprinkle the grated cheddar cheese on top.
11. Return the omelette to the air fryer basket and cook for an additional 1-2 minutes to melt the cheese.
12. Once cooked, remove the omelette from the air fryer and let it cool slightly. Cut the **Vegetable Omelette** into wedges and serve warm.

Beef and Black Bean Stir Fry

Prep: 15 Min | Cook: 10 Min | Serves: 2

Ingredient:

- 300g beef steak, thinly sliced
- 2 tablespoons vegetable oil
- 1 small onion, thinly sliced
- 1 red bell pepper, thinly sliced
- 1 small carrot, thinly sliced
- 100g green beans, trimmed and halved
- 2 cloves garlic, minced
- 2 tablespoons black bean sauce
- 1 tablespoon soy sauce
- 1 teaspoon cornstarch
- Salt and pepper, to taste
- Fresh coriander leaves, for garnish (optional)

Instruction:

1. In a small bowl, mix together the black bean sauce, soy sauce, and cornstarch. Set aside.
2. In Zone 1 of the air fryer basket, add the sliced beef and season with salt and pepper.
3. Select Zone 1 and choose the AIR FRY program. Set the temperature to 200°C and the time to 5 minutes. Press the START/STOP button to begin cooking the beef.
4. In the meantime, heat the vegetable oil in a frying pan or wok over medium heat.
5. Add the sliced onion, bell pepper, carrot, and green beans to the pan. Stir-fry for 3-4 minutes until the vegetables are slightly tender. Add the minced garlic to the pan and stir-fry for an additional 1 minute. Pour the black bean sauce mixture over the vegetables in the pan. Stir well to coat the vegetables.
6. Cook for another 1-2 minutes until the sauce thickens slightly and the vegetables are cooked to your liking.
7. Once the beef is cooked in the air fryer, transfer it to the pan with the vegetables. Stir well to combine.
8. Continue cooking for another 1-2 minutes until the beef is heated through and well coated with the sauce. Remove the pan from heat.
9. Serve the **Beef and Black Bean Stir Fry** hot, garnished with fresh coriander leaves if desire

---

CHAPTER 03: LUNCH

Beef and Tomato Sandwich

Prep: 10 Min | Cook: 10 Min | Serves: 2

Ingredient:

- 300g beef steak, thinly sliced
- 1 tablespoon olive oil
- 1 small onion, thinly sliced
- 1 small red bell pepper, thinly sliced
- 2 large tomatoes, sliced
- 4 slices of bread
- Butter, for spreading
- Salt and pepper, to taste
- Optional toppings: lettuce, cheese, mayonnaise, mustard

Instruction:

1. In a frying pan, heat the olive oil over medium heat. Add the sliced onion and bell pepper to the pan. Sauté for 3-4 minutes until the vegetables are slightly tender. Remove the pan from heat and set aside.
2. Season the beef slices with salt and pepper. Place the seasoned beef slices in Zone 1 of the air fryer basket.
3. Select Zone 1 and choose the AIR FRY program. Set the temperature to 200°C and the time to 8 minutes. Press the START/STOP button to begin cooking the beef.
4. Once the beef is cooked in the air fryer, remove it from Zone 1 and set it aside.
5. Spread butter on one side of each bread slice. Place the buttered bread slices on Zone 2 of the air fryer basket, with the buttered side facing down.
6. Select Zone 2 and choose the AIR FRY program. Set the temperature to 180°C and the time to 2 minutes to toast the bread. Press the START/STOP button to begin toasting the bread.
7. Assemble the sandwich by placing the cooked beef slices, sautéed onions and bell peppers, and sliced tomatoes on one slice of toasted bread. Add any optional toppings you desire.
8. Top with another slice of toasted bread. Cut the **Beef and Tomato Sandwich** in half, if desired, and serve them warm.

Beef and Vegetable Skewers

Prep: 20 Min | Cook: 12 Min | Serves: 4

Ingredient:

- 500g beef steak, cut into 2.5cm cubes
- 1 red bell pepper, cut into 2.5cm pieces
- 1 green bell pepper, cut into 2.5cm pieces
- 1 red onion, cut into 2.5cm pieces
- 250g cherry tomatoes
- 2 tablespoons olive oil
- 2 cloves garlic, minced
- 1 teaspoon dried thyme
- 1 teaspoon paprika
- Salt and pepper, to taste

Instruction:

1. In a bowl, combine the olive oil, minced garlic, dried thyme, paprika, salt, and pepper. Mix well.
2. Thread the beef cubes, bell peppers, red onion, and cherry tomatoes onto skewers, alternating the ingredients.
3. Brush the skewers with the prepared marinade, coating them evenly.
4. Evenly dividing skewers between the two zone, ensuring they are arranged in a single layer.
5. Select Zone 1, choose the AIR FRY program, and set the temperature to 200°C. Set the time to 10-12 minutes. Select MATCH to duplicate settings across both zones. Press the START/STOP button to begin cooking.
6. After 5 minutes of cooking, open the air fryer and carefully rotate the skewers. This ensures even cooking.
7. Close the air fryer and continue cooking for the remaining time or until the beef reaches your desired level of doneness and the vegetables are tender.
8. Once cooked, carefully remove the skewers from the air fryer and let them cool for a few minutes.
9. Serve the **Beef and Vegetable Skewers** hot as a main dish or as part of a meal. They can be enjoyed on their own or paired with rice, salad, or your preferred side dish.

CHAPTER 03: LUNCH

Beef Salad

Prep: 15 Min | Cook: 10 Min | Serves: 4

Ingredient:

- 500g beef steak, thinly sliced
- 200g mixed salad greens
- 1 cucumber, thinly sliced
- 1 red onion, thinly sliced
- 200g cherry tomatoes, halved
- 50g crumbled feta cheese
- 2 tablespoons olive oil
- 2 tablespoons balsamic vinegar
- 1 teaspoon Dijon mustard
- Salt and pepper, to taste

Instruction:

1. In a bowl, whisk together the olive oil, balsamic vinegar, Dijon mustard, salt, and pepper to make the dressing. Set aside.
2. Evenly dividing beef slices between the two zone, ensuring they are arranged in a single layer.
3. Select Zone 1, choose the AIR FRY program, and set the temperature to 200°C. Set the time to 8-10 minutes. Select MATCH to duplicate settings across both zones. Press the START/STOP button to begin cooking.
4. While the beef is cooking, prepare the salad ingredients by combining the mixed salad greens, cucumber slices, red onion slices, cherry tomatoes, and crumbled feta cheese in a large bowl.
5. Once the beef is cooked, remove it from the air fryer and let it rest for a few minutes. Then, slice it into thin strips.
6. Add the sliced beef to the salad bowl and drizzle the dressing over the salad. Toss gently to coat all the ingredients with the dressing.
7. Divide the Beef Salad into four serving plates.
8. Serve the **Beef Salad** as a refreshing and satisfying main dish or as part of a meal.

Beef Stroganoff with Rice

Prep: 15 Min | Cook: 10 Min | Serves: 4

Ingredient:

- 500g beef steak, thinly sliced
- 1 onion, finely chopped
- 200g mushrooms, sliced
- 2 cloves of garlic, minced
- 200ml beef stock
- 200ml double cream
- 2 tablespoons Worcestershire sauce
- 1 tablespoon Dijon mustard
- Salt and pepper, to taste
- Fresh parsley, chopped (for garnish)
- 300g cooked rice (to serve)
- pepper

➤ Instruction:

1. In Zone 1 of the air fryer, place the beef slices and season them with salt and pepper.
2. Select Zone 1, choose the AIR FRY program, and set the temperature to 200°C. Set the time to 8-10 minutes.
3. Press the START/STOP button to begin cooking.
4. In the meantime, heat a pan or skillet on the stovetop over medium heat. Add a little oil and sauté the chopped onion until translucent.
5. Add the sliced mushrooms and minced garlic to the pan. Cook until the mushrooms are tender and any liquid has evaporated.
6. Pour in the beef stock, double cream, Worcestershire sauce, and Dijon mustard. Stir well to combine all the ingredients.
7. Reduce the heat to low and let the sauce simmer for 5-7 minutes, allowing it to thicken slightly. Season with salt and pepper to taste.
8. Once the beef in the air fryer is done, transfer it to the pan with the sauce. Stir well to coat the beef with the sauce. Let it simmer for an additional 2-3 minutes to allow the flavors to meld together.
9. While the beef stroganoff is simmering, cook the rice according to the package instructions.
10. Divide the cooked rice among four serving plates, and spoon the **beef stroganoff** over the rice. Garnish with fresh parsley.

CHAPTER 03: LUNCH

Caesar Salad with Grilled Chicken

Prep: 15 Min | Cook: 15 Min | Serves: 4

Ingredient:

For the Grilled Chicken:
- 500g chicken breast fillets
- 2 tablespoons olive oil
- 2 cloves of garlic, minced
- 1 teaspoon dried thyme
- Salt and pepper, to taste

For the Caesar Salad:
- 200g romaine lettuce, chopped
- 50g grated Parmesan cheese
- 50g croutons
- Caesar dressing (store-bought or homemade)
- Lemon wedges (for serving)

➤ Instruction:

1. In a bowl, combine the olive oil, minced garlic, dried thyme, salt, and pepper. Mix well.
2. Place the chicken breast fillets in Zone 1 of the Ninja Dual Zone Air Fryer.
3. Brush the chicken fillets with the prepared marinade, coating them evenly.
4. Select Zone 1, choose the AIR FRY program, and set the temperature to 200°C. Set the time to 12-15 minutes.
5. Press the START/STOP button to begin cooking.
6. While the chicken is cooking, prepare the Caesar salad by combining the chopped romaine lettuce, grated Parmesan cheese, and croutons in a large bowl.
7. Drizzle Caesar dressing over the salad ingredients and toss gently to coat.
8. Once the chicken is cooked, remove it from the air fryer and let it rest for a few minutes. Then, slice it into thin strips.
9. Divide the Caesar salad among four serving plates. Place the sliced grilled chicken on top of the salad.
10. Serve the **Caesar Salad with Grilled Chicken** alongside cooked rice and lemon wedges.

Cheese Platter

Prep: 10 Min | Cook: 5 Min | Serves: 4

Ingredient:

- 200g Cheddar cheese, sliced
- 200g Brie cheese, sliced
- 200g Blue cheese, crumbled
- 100g Goat cheese, sliced
- 100g Gouda cheese, sliced
- 100g Camembert cheese, sliced
- Assorted crackers and bread slices
- Grapes, for garnish
- Nuts (such as almonds or walnuts), for garnish
- Honey, for drizzling

Instruction:

1. In Zone 1 of the air fryer, place the Cheddar, Brie, Blue cheese, Goat cheese, Gouda, and Camembert cheese slices. You can arrange them in separate sections or mix them together.
2. Select Zone 1, choose the AIR FRY program, and set the temperature to 180°C. Set the time to 5 minutes.
3. Press the START/STOP button to begin cooking.
4. While the cheese is warming in the air fryer, arrange the assorted crackers and bread slices on a serving platter.
5. Once the cheese is warm and slightly melted, remove it from the air fryer and carefully transfer it to the serving platter.
6. Garnish the cheese platter with grapes and nuts for added texture and flavor.
7. Drizzle honey over the cheese for a touch of sweetness.
8. Serve the **Cheese Platter** immediately as an appetizer or part of a gathering.

CHAPTER 03: LUNCH

Chicken and Bacon Pie

Prep: 20 Min | Cook: 30 Min | Serves: 4

Ingredient:

- 500g chicken breast, diced
- 200g bacon, chopped
- 1 onion, finely chopped
- 200g mushrooms, sliced
- 2 cloves of garlic, minced
- 200ml double cream
- 200ml chicken stock
- 1 tablespoon plain flour
- 1 tablespoon butter
- 1 teaspoon dried thyme
- Salt and pepper, to taste
- 500g ready-made puff pastry
- 1 egg, beaten (for egg wash)

Instruction:

1. In pan, cook the bacon until crispy. Remove the bacon using a slotted spoon and set it aside. In the same pan, add the diced chicken and cook until browned.
2. In a separate pan on the stovetop, melt the butter over medium heat. Add the chopped onion and minced garlic, and cook until the onion is translucent. Add the sliced mushrooms to the pan and cook until tender.
3. Sprinkle the flour over the cooked vegetables and stir well to combine. Gradually pour in the chicken stock while stirring continuously to avoid lumps. Stir in the double cream and dried thyme. Season with salt and pepper to taste.
4. Return the cooked bacon and chicken to the pan. Stir everything together and let the mixture simmer for a few minutes until the sauce thickens slightly. Remove from heat and let it cool.
5. Roll out the puff pastry to fit the pie dish. Line the dish with the pastry, ensuring overhang. Pour in the filling and fold overhanging pastry over the top, sealing edges. Cut slits in the top.
6. Brush the pastry with beaten egg for a golden finish.
7. In Zone 1, place the pie dish. Select Zone 1, choose the AIR FRY program, and set the temperature to 180°C. Set the time to 25-30 minutes. Press the START/STOP button to begin cooking.
8. Once the pastry is golden brown and cooked, remove the **Chicken and Bacon Pie** from the air fryer. Let it cool for a few minutes before serving.

Chicken and Spinach Salad

Prep: 15 Min | Cook: 12 Min | Serves: 4

Ingredient:

- 500g chicken breast, sliced
- 200g baby spinach leaves
- 100g cherry tomatoes, halved
- 1 cucumber, sliced
- 1 red onion, thinly sliced
- 50g feta cheese, crumbled
- 50g walnuts, roughly chopped
- 2 tablespoons olive oil
- 2 tablespoons lemon juice
- 1 teaspoon Dijon mustard
- Salt and pepper, to taste

➤ *Instruction:*

1. In a bowl, combine the sliced chicken breast, olive oil, lemon juice, Dijon mustard, salt, and pepper. Mix well to coat the chicken.
2. Evenly dividing marinated chicken slices between the two zone, ensuring they are arranged in a single layer.
3. Select Zone 1, choose the AIR FRY program, and set the temperature to 200°C. Set the time to 10-12 minutes. Select MATCH to duplicate settings across both zones. Press the START/STOP button to begin cooking.
4. While the chicken is cooking, prepare the salad by combining the baby spinach leaves, cherry tomatoes, cucumber slices, red onion slices, crumbled feta cheese, and chopped walnuts in a large salad bowl.
5. In a separate small bowl, whisk together the olive oil, lemon juice, Dijon mustard, salt, and pepper to create the salad dressing.
6. Once the chicken is cooked, remove it from the air fryer and let it rest for a few minutes. Then, slice it into thin strips. Add the sliced chicken to the salad bowl and drizzle the dressing over the salad ingredients. Toss the salad gently to ensure everything is coated in the dressing.
7. Serve the **Chicken and Spinach Salad** immediately as a refreshing and healthy meal.

CHAPTER 03: LUNCH

Chicken Burger

Prep: 15 Min | Cook: 15 Min | Serves: 4

Ingredient:

For the chicken patties:
- 500g ground chicken
- 1 small onion, finely chopped
- 2 cloves of garlic, minced
- 1 tablespoon fresh parsley, chopped
- 1 teaspoon dried thyme
- 1 teaspoon paprika
- Salt and pepper, to taste

For assembling the burger:
- 4 burger buns
- Lettuce leaves
- Tomato slices
- Red onion slices
- Pickles (optional)
- Condiments of your choice (such as mayonnaise, ketchup, or mustard)

➤ *Instruction:*

1. In a mixing bowl, combine the ground chicken, chopped onion, minced garlic, fresh parsley, dried thyme, paprika, salt, and pepper. Mix well until all the ingredients are evenly combined.
2. Divide the chicken mixture into 4 equal portions and shape them into patties.
3. Evenly dividing chicken patties between the two zone, ensuring they are arranged in a single layer.
4. Select Zone 1, choose the AIR FRY program, and set the temperature to 200°C. Set the time to 12-15 minutes. Select MATCH to duplicate settings across both zones. Press the START/STOP button to begin cooking.
5. While the chicken patties are cooking, prepare the burger buns and toppings. Slice the burger buns in half and lightly toast them, if desired. Wash and prepare the lettuce leaves, tomato slices, red onion slices, pickles, and any condiments you prefer.
6. Once the chicken patties are cooked and reach an internal temperature of 75°C, remove them from the air fryer and let them rest for a few minutes.
7. Assemble the burgers by placing a chicken patty on the bottom half of each bun. Top it with lettuce, tomato slices, red onion slices, pickles, and your preferred condiments.
8. Place the top half of the bun on the assembled burger, and your **Chicken Burger** is ready to serve.

Chicken Katsu Curry

Prep: 20 Min | Cook: 15 Min | Serves: 4

Ingredient:

For the chicken:
- 500g chicken breast, boneless and skinless
- 100g all-purpose flour
- 2 eggs, beaten
- 150g panko breadcrumbs
- Salt and pepper, to taste

For the curry sauce:
- 1 onion, finely chopped
- 2 cloves of garlic, minced
- 1 carrot, diced
- 1 potato, diced
- 2 tablespoons curry powder
- 500ml chicken or vegetable stock
- 2 tablespoons vegetable oil
- Salt, to taste

Instruction:

1. Slice the chicken breast into thin, even pieces.
2. Set up three separate shallow bowls for the breading process. In one bowl, place the flour. In the second bowl, add the beaten eggs. In the third bowl, place the panko breadcrumbs.
3. Season the chicken slices with salt and pepper. Dredge each chicken slice in flour, then dip it into the beaten eggs, ensuring it is fully coated. Finally, press the chicken slice into the panko breadcrumbs, making sure it is evenly coated. Repeat for all the chicken slices.
4. Evenly dividing breaded chicken slices between the two zone, ensuring they are arranged in a single layer.
5. Select Zone 1, choose the AIR FRY program, and set the temperature to 200°C. Set the time to 12-15 minutes. Select MATCH. Press the START/STOP.
6. While chicken cooks, make curry sauce by sautéing onion and garlic in oil. Add carrot, potato, curry powder and stock. Simmer until vegetables are tender.
7. Once the chicken is cooked and golden brown, remove it from the air fryer and let it rest for a few minutes.
8. Slice the cooked chicken into strips.
9. Serve the **chicken katsu** alongside cooked rice and the curry sauce. Garnish with fresh coriander and pickles, if desired.

CHAPTER 03: LUNCH

Chicken Pasta

Prep: 15 Min | Cook: 25 Min | Serves: 4

Ingredient:

- 300g penne pasta
- 500g chicken breast, diced
- 1 onion, finely chopped
- 2 cloves of garlic, minced
- 200g mushrooms, sliced
- 1 red bell pepper, diced
- 400g canned chopped tomatoes
- 2 tablespoons tomato paste
- 1 teaspoon dried oregano
- 1 teaspoon dried basil
- Salt and pepper, to taste
- Grated Parmesan cheese, for serving
- Fresh basil leaves, for garnish

Instruction:

1. Cook the penne pasta according to the package instructions until al dente. Drain and set aside.
2. In Zone 1 of the air fryer, place the diced chicken breast, chopped onion, minced garlic, sliced mushrooms, and diced red bell pepper.
3. Select Zone 1, choose the AIR FRY program, and set the temperature to 200°C. Set the time to 10-12 minutes.
4. Press the START/STOP button to begin cooking.
5. While the chicken and vegetables are cooking, prepare the sauce. In a separate pan on the stovetop, heat a little oil over medium heat.
6. Add the canned chopped tomatoes, tomato paste, dried oregano, dried basil, salt, and pepper to the pan. Stir well and let the sauce simmer for about 10 minutes, allowing the flavors to meld together.
7. Once the chicken and vegetables are cooked, combine them with the pasta in a large bowl.
8. Pour the tomato sauce over the pasta and chicken mixture. Toss well to coat everything evenly.
9. Serve the **Chicken Pasta** hot, garnished with grated Parmesan cheese and fresh basil leaves.

Empanadas

Prep: 30 Min | Cook: 15 Min | Serves: 4-6

Ingredient:

For the dough:
- 300g plain flour
- 150g unsalted butter, chilled and diced
- 1 teaspoon salt
- 6-8 tablespoons cold water

For the filling:
- 300g ground beef
- 1 onion, finely chopped
- 2 cloves of garlic, minced
- 1 red bell pepper, diced
- 1 teaspoon ground cumin
- 1 teaspoon paprika
- Salt and pepper, to taste
- 2 tablespoons olive oil

For sealing and glazing:
- 1 egg, beaten

Instruction:

1. Make the dough by mixing flour, salt, chilled diced butter and water until it comes together. Form the dough into a ball and cover it with plastic wrap. Refrigerate for 15-20 minutes.
2. In the meantime, prepare the filling. Heat the olive oil in a pan over medium heat. Add the chopped onion, minced garlic, and diced red bell pepper. Sauté until the vegetables are softened.
3. Add the ground beef to the pan and cook until browned. Stir in the ground cumin, paprika, salt, and pepper. Cook for an additional 2-3 minutes. Remove from heat and set aside.
4. Remove the dough from the refrigerator and roll it out on a lightly floured surface until it is about 3-4mm thick. Use a round cutter (approximately 10cm in diameter) to cut out circles from the dough.
5. Place a spoonful of the filling in the center of each dough circle. Fold the dough over to create a half-moon shape. Use a fork to press and seal the edges.
6. Evenly dividing empanadas between the two zone, ensuring they are arranged in a single layer. Brush the beaten egg over the empanadas for a glaze.
7. Select Zone 1, choose the AIR FRY program, and set the temperature to 180°C. Set the time to 12-15 minutes. Select MATCH. Press the START/STOP. Once the **empanadas** are golden brown and crispy, remove them from the air fryer and let them cool for a few minutes before serving.

CHAPTER 03: LUNCH

Ham and Cheese Toastie

Prep: 10 Min | Cook: 8 Min | Serves: 4

Ingredient:

- 8 slices of bread
- 200g sliced ham
- 200g cheddar cheese, grated
- Butter, softened

Instruction:

1. Lay out the slices of bread on a clean surface. Spread a thin layer of softened butter on one side of each slice.
2. Place the ham slices on four slices of bread, dividing it evenly among them.
3. Sprinkle the grated cheddar cheese over the ham, again dividing it evenly.
4. Place the other four slices of bread on top, buttered side facing up, to form sandwiches.
5. Evenly dividing sandwiches between the two zone, ensuring they are arranged in a single layer.
6. Select Zone 1, choose the AIR FRY program, and set the temperature to 180°C. Set the time to 6-8 minutes. Select MATCH to duplicate settings across both zones. Press the START/STOP button to begin cooking.
7. After 3-4 minutes, carefully flip the sandwiches to ensure even browning.
8. Continue cooking for another 3-4 minutes until the bread is golden brown and the cheese is melted.
9. Once done, remove the **Ham and Cheese Toasties** from the air fryer and let them cool for a minute or two before serving.

Halloumi Burger

Prep: 10 Min | Cook: 10 Min | Serves: 4

Ingredient:

- 250g halloumi cheese, sliced
- 4 burger buns
- 1 large tomato, sliced
- 1 small red onion, thinly sliced
- Lettuce leaves
- 4 tablespoons mayonnaise
- 2 tablespoons ketchup
- 1 tablespoon olive oil
- Salt and pepper, to taste

➤ Instruction:

1. In a small bowl, mix together the mayonnaise and ketchup to create a sauce. Set aside.
2. In Zone 1 of the air fryer, place the halloumi cheese slices. Drizzle the olive oil over the cheese slices.
3. Select Zone 1, choose the AIR FRY program, and set the temperature to 200°C. Set the time to 8-10 minutes.
4. Press the START/STOP button to begin cooking.
5. While the halloumi is cooking, prepare the burger buns and toppings. Slice the burger buns in half and lightly toast them.
6. Spread the sauce mixture on the bottom halves of the burger buns.
7. Layer the lettuce leaves, tomato slices, and red onion slices on top of the sauce.
8. Once the halloumi is cooked and has a golden brown color, remove it from the air fryer.
9. Place the halloumi slices on top of the prepared burger buns.
10. Season with salt and pepper to taste.
11. Place the top halves of the burger buns on the halloumi to complete the **burgers**.

CHAPTER 03: LUNCH

Halloumi Sticks

Prep: 10 Min | Cook: 10 Min | Serves: 4

Ingredient:

- 250g halloumi cheese
- 2 tablespoons plain flour
- 1 teaspoon paprika
- 1/2 teaspoon garlic powder
- 1/4 teaspoon black pepper
- Olive oil spray, for coating

➤ Instruction:

1. Cut the halloumi cheese into sticks, approximately 1cm in width and 7-8cm in length.
2. In a shallow bowl, mix together the plain flour, paprika, garlic powder, and black pepper.
3. Coat each halloumi stick in the flour mixture, ensuring they are evenly coated.
4. In Zone 1 of the air fryer, place the halloumi sticks in a single layer, leaving space between each stick.
5. Select Zone 1, choose the AIR FRY program, and set the temperature to 200°C. Set the time to 8-10 minutes.
6. Press the START/STOP button to begin cooking.
7. After 4-5 minutes of cooking, open the air fryer and gently shake the basket to ensure even cooking.
8. Close the air fryer and continue cooking for another 4-5 minutes or until the halloumi sticks are golden brown and crispy.
9. Once done, remove the **Halloumi Sticks** from the air fryer and let them cool for a minute or two before serving.

Jacket Potatoes

Prep: 5 Min | Cook: 50 Min | Serves: 4

Ingredient:

- 4 large baking potatoes
- Olive oil, for brushing
- Salt, to taste
- Optional toppings: butter, grated cheese, sour cream, chives

Instruction:

1. Scrub the potatoes clean under running water. Pat the potatoes dry with a paper towel.
2. Use a fork to pierce the potatoes several times on all sides. This allows steam to escape during cooking.
3. Brush the potatoes with olive oil, ensuring they are evenly coated.
4. Sprinkle salt over the potatoes, to taste.
5. Place the potatoes in Zone 1 of the air fryer basket.
6. Select Zone 1, choose the AIR FRY program, and set the temperature to 200°C. Set the time to 50 minutes, depending on the size of the potatoes and desired level of doneness. Press the START/STOP.
7. Halfway through the cooking time, use tongs to carefully flip the potatoes to ensure even cooking.
8. Remove the Jacket Potatoes from the air fryer using oven mitts or tongs. Carefully slice open each potato, and fluff the insides with a fork.
9. Serve the Jacket Potatoes hot with your choice of toppings, such as butter, grated cheese, sour cream, or chives.
10. Enjoy the delicious and comforting **Jacket Potatoes** as a versatile and satisfying meal option.

CHAPTER 03: LUNCH

Margherita Pizza

Prep: 15 Min | Cook: 12 Min | Serves: 2-3

Ingredient:

- 1 ready-made pizza dough (approximately 300g)
- 150g passata (strained tomatoes)
- 150g mozzarella cheese, sliced
- Fresh basil leaves
- Olive oil
- Salt and pepper, to taste

Instruction:

1. Roll out the pizza dough on a floured surface to your desired thickness. Aim for a circle approximately 25cm in diameter.
2. Carefully transfer the rolled-out dough to a piece of parchment paper that fits the size of your air fryer basket.
3. Spread the passata evenly over the dough, leaving a small border around the edges for the crust.
4. Arrange the mozzarella slices on top of the passata, covering the pizza evenly.
5. Tear a few fresh basil leaves and scatter them over the cheese.
6. Drizzle a little olive oil over the pizza. Season with salt and pepper to taste.
7. In Zone 1 of the air fryer, place the pizza (with the parchment paper) in a single layer.
8. Select Zone 1, choose the AIR FRY program, and set the temperature to 200°C. Set the time to 10-12 minutes.
9. Press the START/STOP button to begin cooking.
10. After 5-6 minutes of cooking, open the air fryer and rotate the pizza to ensure even browning.
11. Close the air fryer and continue cooking for another 5-6 minutes or until the crust is golden brown and the cheese is melted and bubbly.
12. Once done, carefully remove the **Margherita Pizza** from the air fryer using tongs or a spatula. Let it cool for a few minutes before slicing and serving.

Meatballs

Prep: 15 Min | Cook: 15 Min | Serves: 4

Ingredient:

- 500g ground beef
- 1 small onion, finely chopped
- 2 cloves garlic, minced
- 25gbreadcrumbs
- 28g grated Parmesan cheese
- 1 egg
- 1 tablespoon chopped fresh parsley
- 1 teaspoon dried oregano
- 1/2 teaspoon salt
- 1/4 teaspoon black pepper

Instruction:

1. In a large bowl, combine the ground beef, onion, garlic, breadcrumbs, Parmesan cheese, egg, parsley, dried oregano, salt, and black pepper. Mix well until all the ingredients are evenly combined.
2. Shape the mixture into meatballs, about 3cm in diameter. You should have approximately 16 meatballs.
3. Evenly dividing meatballs between the two zone in a single layer, leaving space between each meatball.
4. Select Zone 1, choose the AIR FRY program, and set the temperature to 200°C. Set the time to 12-15 minutes. Select MATCH to duplicate settings across both zones. Press the START/STOP button to begin cooking.
5. After 6-8 minutes of cooking, open the air fryer and shake the basket or use tongs to turn the meatballs for even browning.
6. Close the air fryer and continue cooking for another 6-8 minutes or until the meatballs are cooked through and browned on the outside.
7. Once done, remove the **Meatballs** from the air fryer and let them cool for a few minutes before serving.

CHAPTER 03: LUNCH

Pizza Pockets

Prep: 15 Min | Cook: 12 Min | Serves: 4

Ingredient:

- 1 sheet ready-made puff pastry, thawed
- 100g pizza sauce or tomato passata
- 100g shredded mozzarella cheese
- 50g sliced pepperoni or your preferred pizza toppings
- 1 egg, beaten (for egg wash)
- Dried oregano or Italian seasoning, for garnish

Instruction:

1. Roll out the puff pastry sheet on a lightly floured surface to a thickness of about 3mm.
2. Using a knife or pizza cutter, cut the puff pastry into 4 equal squares.
3. Spoon approximately 1 tablespoon of pizza sauce onto the center of each puff pastry square, leaving a small border around the edges.
4. Sprinkle shredded mozzarella cheese over the sauce, and add your desired pizza toppings, such as sliced pepperoni.
5. Fold each puff pastry square diagonally to form a triangle, enclosing the filling. Press the edges firmly to seal.
6. Place the pizza pockets in Zone 1 of the air fryer, ensuring they are not touching each other. Brush the tops of the pizza pockets with beaten egg to create a golden crust.
7. Select Zone 1, choose the AIR FRY program, and set the temperature to 200°C. Set the time to 10-12 minutes.
8. Press the START/STOP button to begin cooking.
9. After 5-6 minutes of cooking, open the air fryer and gently flip the pizza pockets over using tongs or a spatula.
10. Close the air fryer and continue cooking for another 5-6 minutes or until the pizza pockets are puffed up and golden brown.
11. Once done, remove the **Pizza Pockets** from the air fryer. Sprinkle dried oregano or Italian seasoning over the top for added flavor.

Pork Sandwich

Prep: 10 Min | Cook: 12 Min | Serves: 4

Ingredient:

- 350g pork tenderloin
- 1 tablespoon olive oil
- 1 teaspoon smoked paprika
- 1 teaspoon garlic powder
- 1/2 teaspoon dried thyme
- Salt and pepper, to taste
- 4 bread rolls or buns
- Lettuce leaves
- Sliced tomatoes
- Sliced red onion
- Condiments of your choice (mayonnaise, mustard, etc.)

▶ *Instruction:*

1. Trim any excess fat from the pork tenderloin and slice it into 1.5cm thick medallions.
2. In a bowl, combine the olive oil, smoked paprika, garlic powder, dried thyme, salt, and pepper. Mix well to create a marinade.
3. Add the pork medallions to the marinade, ensuring they are evenly coated. Let them marinate for 5-10 minutes.
4. In Zone 1 of the air fryer, place the pork medallions in a single layer, leaving space between each piece.
5. Select Zone 1, choose the AIR FRY program, and set the temperature to 200°C. Set the time to 10-12 minutes.
6. Press the START/STOP button to begin cooking.
7. After 5-6 minutes of cooking, open the air fryer and flip the pork medallions over using tongs.
8. Close the air fryer and continue cooking for another 5-6 minutes or until the pork is cooked through and nicely browned.
9. Once done, remove the pork medallions from the air fryer and let them rest for a few minutes.
10. Assemble your sandwiches by placing lettuce leaves, sliced tomatoes, and sliced red onion on the bread rolls or buns. Add the cooked pork medallions.
11. Add your preferred condiments, such as mayonnaise or mustard.
12. Serve the **Pork Sandwiches** immediately and enjoy!

CHAPTER 03: LUNCH

Pork Wrap

Prep: 10 Min | Cook: 25 Min | Serves: 4

Ingredient:

- 400g pork tenderloin
- 1 tablespoon olive oil
- 1 teaspoon smoked paprika
- 1 teaspoon garlic powder
- 1/2 teaspoon dried thyme
- Salt and pepper, to taste
- 4 large tortilla wraps
- Shredded lettuce
- Sliced tomatoes
- Sliced red onion
- Sliced cucumber
- Greek yogurt or mayonnaise (optional)
- Hot sauce or salsa (optional)

▶ *Instruction:*

1. Trim any excess fat from the pork tenderloin and slice it into thin strips.
2. In a bowl, combine the olive oil, smoked paprika, garlic powder, dried thyme, salt, and pepper. Mix well to create a marinade.
3. Add the pork strips to the marinade, ensuring they are evenly coated. Let them marinate for 5-10 minutes.
4. Evenly dividing marinated pork strips between the two zone in a single layer, leaving space between each piece.
5. Select Zone 1, choose the AIR FRY program, and set the temperature to 200°C. Set the time to 10-12 minutes. Select MATCH. Press the START/STOP button to begin cooking.
6. After 5-6 minutes of cooking, open the air fryer and flip the pork strips over using tongs.
7. Once done, remove the pork strips from the air fryer and let them rest for a few minutes.
8. Warm the tortilla wraps in a dry skillet or microwave.
9. Assemble your wraps by placing a handful of shredded lettuce, sliced tomatoes, sliced red onion, and sliced cucumber on each tortilla wrap. Add the cooked pork strips to each wrap.
10. If desired, drizzle Greek yogurt or mayonnaise over the fillings and add hot sauce or salsa for extra flavor.
11. Fold the sides of the tortilla wraps inward and roll them up tightly.
12. Serve the **Pork Wraps** immediately and enjoy!

Prawn Cocktail Stuffed Avocado

Prep: 15 Min | Cook: 5 Min | Serves: 4

Ingredient:

- 4 ripe avocados
- 200g cooked prawns
- 4 tablespoons mayonnaise
- 1 tablespoon ketchup
- 1 teaspoon Worcestershire sauce
- 1 teaspoon lemon juice
- Salt and pepper, to taste
- Lettuce leaves, for serving
- Lemon wedges, for serving
- Fresh dill or parsley, for garnish

➤ Instruction:

1. Cut the avocados in half lengthwise. Remove the pits and scoop out a small portion of the avocado flesh from each half, creating a hollow space for the prawn cocktail filling. Set aside the scooped-out avocado flesh for later use.
2. In a bowl, combine the cooked prawns, mayonnaise, ketchup, Worcestershire sauce, lemon juice, salt, and pepper. Mix well to coat the prawns with the sauce.
3. Evenly dividing stuffed avocados between the two zone, cut side up.
4. Select Zone 1, choose the AIR FRY program, and set the temperature to 180°C. Set the time to 5 minutes. Select MATCH. Press the START/STOP button to begin cooking.
5. Fill each hollowed avocado half with the prawn cocktail mixture, dividing it evenly among the avocados.
6. Place lettuce leaves on a serving platter and arrange the **stuffed avocado** halves on top.
7. Garnish with fresh dill or parsley and serve with lemon wedges on the side.

CHAPTER 03: LUNCH

Roasted Chickpeas

Prep: 5 Min | Cook: 20 Min | Serves: 4

Ingredient:

- 400g canned chickpeas, drained and rinsed
- 1 tablespoon olive oil
- 1 teaspoon smoked paprika
- 1/2 teaspoon ground cumin
- 1/2 teaspoon garlic powder
- 1/2 teaspoon salt
- 1/4 teaspoon black pepper
- Optional: additional spices or seasonings of your choice (such as chili powder, curry powder, or dried herbs)

➤ Instruction:

1. In a bowl, combine the drained and rinsed chickpeas, olive oil, smoked paprika, ground cumin, garlic powder, salt, and black pepper. Toss well to coat the chickpeas evenly.
2. In Zone 1 of the air fryer, spread the seasoned chickpeas in a single layer.
3. Select Zone 1, choose the ROAST program, and set the temperature to 200°C. Set the time to 15-20 minutes.
4. Press the START/STOP button to begin cooking.
5. After 10 minutes of cooking, open the air fryer and shake the basket or use tongs to toss the chickpeas for even cooking.
6. Close the air fryer and continue cooking for another 5-10 minutes or until the chickpeas are golden brown and crispy. Keep an eye on them as cooking times may vary.
7. Once done, remove the roasted chickpeas from the air fryer and let them cool slightly before serving.
8. Serve the **Roasted Chickpeas** as a delicious crunchy snack or as a topping for salads or soups.

Savoury Muffins

Prep: 15 Min | Cook: 20 Min | Serves: 6

Ingredient:

- 200g self-raising flour
- 1 teaspoon baking powder
- 1/2 teaspoon salt
- 1/4 teaspoon black pepper
- 100g grated cheddar cheese
- 100g cooked ham, diced
- 1 small red bell pepper, finely chopped
- 2 spring onions, finely chopped
- 150ml milk
- 2 tablespoons vegetable oil
- 2 eggs

➤ Instruction:

1. In a large bowl, whisk together the self-raising flour, baking powder, salt, and black pepper.
2. Add the grated cheddar cheese, cooked ham, red bell pepper, and spring onions to the bowl. Mix well to combine.
3. In a separate bowl, whisk together the milk, vegetable oil, and eggs.
4. Pour the wet ingredients into the dry ingredients. Stir gently until just combined. Do not overmix.
5. In Zone 1 of the air fryer, place 6 muffin cases or silicone muffin molds.
6. Spoon the muffin batter evenly into the muffin cases or molds.
7. Select Zone 1, choose the AIR FRY program, and set the temperature to 180°C. Set the time to 15-18 minutes.
8. Press the START/STOP button to begin cooking.
9. After 10-12 minutes of cooking, open the air fryer and check the muffins. If they are lightly golden and a toothpick inserted into the center comes out clean, they are done. If not, continue cooking for a few more minutes.
10. Once done, remove the muffins from the air fryer and let them cool slightly before serving.
11. Serve the **Savoury Muffins** warm. They can be enjoyed as a snack or as part of a meal.

CHAPTER 03: LUNCH

Tofu Stir Fry

Prep: 20 Min | Cook: 15 Min | Serves: 4

Ingredient:

- 400g firm tofu, drained and pressed
- 2 tablespoons soy sauce
- 1 tablespoon sesame oil
- 2 cloves garlic, minced
- 2 cm piece of ginger, grated
- 1 onion, sliced
- 1 red bell pepper, sliced
- 150g snap peas, trimmed
- 150g mushrooms, sliced
- 2 spring onions, chopped (for garnish)
- 1 tablespoon sesame seeds (for garnish)
- Cooked rice or noodles, for serving

➤ Instruction:

1. Cut the pressed tofu into bite-sized cubes.
2. In a bowl, combine the soy sauce, sesame oil, minced garlic, and grated ginger. Add the tofu cubes and gently toss to coat them in the marinade. Let it marinate for 10 minutes.
3. In Zone 1 of the air fryer, place the marinated tofu cubes in a single layer.
4. Select Zone 1, choose the AIR FRY program, and set the temperature to 200°C. Set the time to 15 minutes.
5. Press the START/STOP button to begin cooking.
6. While the tofu is cooking, heat a small amount of oil in a pan or wok on the stovetop. Add the sliced onion, red bell pepper, snap peas, and mushrooms. Stir-fry over medium-high heat until the vegetables are tender-crisp.
7. Once the tofu is done in the air fryer, add it to the stir-fried vegetables and toss gently to combine.
8. Serve the **Tofu Stir Fry** over cooked rice or noodles.
9. Garnish with chopped spring onions and sesame seeds.

Tortilla Chips

Prep: 5 Min | Cook: 10 Min | Serves: 4

Ingredient:

- 4 large tortilla wraps
- 1 tablespoon olive oil
- 1/2 teaspoon salt
- Optional: additional seasonings such as chili powder, paprika, or garlic powder

Instruction:

1. Stack the tortilla wraps on top of each other and cut them into triangle shapes, about 8 triangles per wrap.
2. In a bowl, combine the olive oil and salt. If desired, add any additional seasonings of your choice and mix well.
3. Evenly dividing tortilla triangles between the two zone.
4. Select Zone 1, choose the AIR FRY program, and set the temperature to 180°C. Set the time to 8-10 minutes. Select MATCH to duplicate settings across both zones. Press the START/STOP button to begin cooking.
5. After 4-5 minutes of cooking, open the air fryer and shake the basket or use tongs to toss the tortilla triangles for even cooking.
6. Close the air fryer and continue cooking for another 3-5 minutes or until the tortilla chips are golden brown and crispy. Keep an eye on them as cooking times may vary.
7. Once done, remove the tortilla chips from the air fryer and let them cool slightly before serving.
8. Serve the **Tortilla Chips** as a snack or as a side dish with salsa, guacamole, or your favorite dip.

CHAPTER 03: LUNCH

Vegetable Curry with Naan Bread

Prep: 15 Min | Cook: 20 Min | Serves: 4

Ingredient:

Vegetable Curry Ingredients:
- 2 tablespoons vegetable oil
- 1 onion, diced
- 2 cloves garlic, minced
- 2 cm piece of ginger, grated
- 1 red bell pepper, sliced
- 1 zucchini, sliced
- 200g cauliflower florets
- 200g carrots, sliced
- 400g canned chopped tomatoes
- 400ml coconut milk
- 2 tablespoons curry powder
- 1 teaspoon ground cumin
- 1 teaspoon ground coriander
- Salt and pepper, to taste
- Fresh coriander leaves, for garnish

Naan Bread Ingredients:
- 250g plain flour
- 1 teaspoon baking powder
- 1/2 teaspoon salt
- 150g plain yogurt
- 2 tablespoons vegetable oil
- 2 tablespoons melted butter
- Optional: garlic or nigella seeds for topping

Instruction:

1. In Zone 1 place the cauliflower florets and carrots. Select Zone 1, choose the AIR FRY program, and set the temperature to 180°C. Set the time to 15 minutes. Press the START/STOP.
2. Meanwhile, Sauté onion, garlic and ginger in oil. Add peppers, zucchini and spices. Pour in tomatoes and coconut milk. Simmer 10 minutes, allowing the flavors to meld together.
3. After 15 minutes, open the air fryer and check the cauliflower florets and carrots. They should be partially cooked.
4. While the curry is simmering, prepare the Naan bread. In a mixing bowl, combine the plain flour, baking powder, and salt. Add the plain yogurt and vegetable oil. Mix well until a dough forms.
5. Divide the dough into 4 equal portions and roll each portion into a round or oval shape, about 0.5 cm thick.
6. In Zone 2, place the Naan bread. Select Zone 2, choose the AIR FRY program, and set the temperature to 180°C. Set the time to 5-6 minutes. Press the START/STOP. After 2-3 minutes, open the air fryer and flip the Naan bread. Brush the tops with melted butter and sprinkle with garlic or nigella seeds if desired. Close the air fryer and continue cooking for another 2-3 minutes or until the Naan bread is golden and slightly puffed.
7. Combine the pre-cooked cauliflower florets and carrots with the simmering curry sauce, stir gently to combine, and continue simmering until all the vegetables are tender and cooked through, then serve with freshly cooked **Naan bread**.

Vegetable Fritters

Prep: 10 Min | Cook: 15 Min | Serves: 4

Ingredient:

- 200g self-raising flour
- 1 teaspoon baking powder
- 1/2 teaspoon salt
- 1/2 teaspoon ground cumin
- 1/2 teaspoon paprika
- 1/4 teaspoon turmeric
- 150ml milk
- 1 egg
- 200g mixed vegetables (e.g., grated courgette, grated carrot, sweetcorn kernels, diced bell peppers)
- Vegetable oil spray

Instruction:

1. In a mixing bowl, combine the self-raising flour, baking powder, salt, ground cumin, paprika, and turmeric.
2. In a separate bowl, whisk together the milk and egg until well combined.
3. Gradually pour the milk and egg mixture into the dry ingredients, stirring until a smooth batter forms.
4. Add the mixed vegetables to the batter and stir until they are evenly distributed.
5. In Zone 1 of the air fryer, place spoonfuls of the vegetable batter to form fritter patties, leaving a little space between each.
6. Select Zone 1, choose the AIR FRY program, and set the temperature to 200°C. Set the time to 12-15 minutes.
7. Press the START/STOP button to begin cooking.
8. After 6-7 minutes of cooking, open the air fryer and spray the fritters with vegetable oil spray. This will help them crisp up.
9. Close the air fryer and continue cooking for another 6-8 minutes or until the fritters are golden brown and crispy.
10. Once done, remove the vegetable fritters from the air fryer and transfer them to a plate lined with kitchen paper to absorb any excess oil.
11. Serve the **Vegetable Fritters** as a snack or as a side dish with your favorite dipping sauce.

CHAPTER 01: CAKES

Vegetable Paella

Prep: 10 Min | Cook: 30 Min | Serves: 4tties

Ingredient:

- 200g paella rice
- 1 onion, diced
- 1 red bell pepper, diced
- 1 yellow bell pepper, diced
- 2 cloves of garlic, minced
- 200g cherry tomatoes, halved
- 100g frozen peas
- 600ml vegetable stock
- 2 tbsp olive oil
- 1 tsp smoked paprika
- 1/2 tsp turmeric
- Salt and pepper, to taste
- Fresh parsley, chopped (for garnish)
- Lemon wedges (for serving)

Instruction:

1. In Zone 1 of the Ninja Dual Zone Air Fryer, add the diced onion, diced red bell pepper, diced yellow bell pepper, and minced garlic. Drizzle with olive oil.
2. In Zone 2, add the paella rice.
3. Select Zone 1, choose the AIR FRY program, and set the temperature to 180°C. Set the time to 10 minutes. Select MATCH. Press the START/STOP button to begin air frying the vegetable mixture and rice.
4. While the vegetables and rice are cooking, in a separate pot, heat the vegetable stock until simmering.
5. After 10 minutes of air frying, carefully remove the vegetable mixture and rice from the air fryer.
6. In a large pan or skillet, combine the cooked vegetable mixture and rice. Add the cherry tomatoes, frozen peas, smoked paprika, turmeric, and season with salt and pepper. Mix everything together. Pour the simmering vegetable stock into the pan with the vegetable mixture and rice. Stir to combine.
7. Place the pan back into Zone 1. Select Zone 1, choose the AIR FRY program, and set the temperature to 180°C. Set the time to 20 minutes. Press the START/STOP button to begin air frying the Vegetable Paella.
8. After 20 minutes, carefully remove the **Vegetable Paella** from the air fryer. Garnish with fresh parsley and serve hot.

Bang Bang Shrimp

Prep: 15 Min | Cook: 10 Min | Serves: 4

Ingredient:

- 400g raw shrimp, peeled and deveined
- 100g cornstarch
- 2 large eggs, beaten
- 50g panko breadcrumbs
- 1 teaspoon paprika
- 1/2 teaspoon garlic powder
- 1/2 teaspoon salt
- 1/4 teaspoon black pepper
- 1/4 teaspoon cayenne pepper (adjust according to spice preference)

For the Bang Bang Sauce:
- 4 tablespoons mayonnaise
- 2 tablespoons sweet chili sauce
- 1 tablespoon honey
- 1 tablespoon lime juice
- 1/2 teaspoon Sriracha sauce (adjust according to spice preference)

Instruction:

1. In three separate bowls, set up a breading station. In the first bowl, place the cornstarch. In the second bowl, beat the eggs. In the third bowl, combine the panko breadcrumbs, paprika, garlic powder, salt, black pepper, and cayenne pepper.
2. Dip each shrimp into the cornstarch, then into the beaten eggs, and finally coat it in the breadcrumb mixture. Press gently to adhere the breadcrumbs to the shrimp. Repeat for all the shrimp.
3. Evenly dividing breaded shrimp between the two zone, ensuring they are arranged in a single layer.
4. Select Zone 1, choose the AIR FRY program, and set the temperature to 200°C. Set the time to 10 minutes. Select MATCH to duplicate settings across both zones. Press the START/STOP button to begin cooking.
5. While the shrimp are cooking, prepare the Bang Bang Sauce by whisking together mayonnaise, sweet chili sauce, honey, lime juice, and Sriracha sauce in a bowl. Adjust the Sriracha sauce according to your spice preference.
6. Once the cooking time is up, remove the shrimp from the air fryer and let them cool for a few minutes.
7. Serve the **Bang Bang Shrimp** with the prepared Bang Bang Sauce as a dipping sauce.

CHAPTER 04: DINNER/SUPPER

BBQ Pulled Pork

Prep: 10 Min | Cook: 75 Min | Serves: 6

Ingredient:

- 1 kg pork shoulder, boneless
- 1 onion, chopped
- 3 cloves of garlic, minced
- 250 ml BBQ sauce
- 2 tbsp brown sugar
- 2 tbsp apple cider vinegar
- 1 tbsp Worcestershire sauce
- 1 tsp smoked paprika
- 1/2 tsp chili powder
- Salt and pepper, to taste
- 4 burger buns
- Coleslaw (optional, for serving)

Instruction:

1. In Zone 1, place the chopped onion and minced garlic. In Zone 2, place the pork shoulder.
2. Select Zone 1, choose the AIR FRY program, and set the temperature to 140°C. Set the time to 1 hour. Select MATCH. Press the START/STOP button to begin air frying the onion, garlic, and pork shoulder.
3. While the pork is air frying, in a separate bowl, mix together the BBQ sauce, brown sugar, apple cider vinegar, Worcestershire sauce, smoked paprika, chili powder, salt, and pepper to create the BBQ sauce.
4. After 1 hour of air frying, carefully remove the onion, garlic, and pork shoulder from the air fryer.
5. Use two forks to shred the pork shoulder into smaller pieces.
6. Place the shredded pork shoulder in Zone 1 of the air fryer.
7. Pour the prepared BBQ sauce over the shredded pork shoulder.
8. Select Zone 1, choose the AIR FRY program, and set the temperature to 140°C. Set the time to 15 minutes. Press the START/STOP button to begin air frying the BBQ Pulled Pork.
9. While the pork is air frying, prepare the burger buns and optional coleslaw for serving.
10. After 15 minutes, carefully remove the BBQ Pulled Pork from the air fryer. Serve the **BBQ Pulled Pork** on the burger buns, topped with coleslaw if desired.

BBQ Ribs

Prep: 10 Min | Cook: 60 Min | Serves: 4-6

Ingredient:

- 1.5 kg pork ribs
- 200 ml BBQ sauce
- 2 tbsp brown sugar
- 2 tbsp apple cider vinegar
- 1 tbsp Worcestershire sauce
- 1 tsp smoked paprika
- 1/2 tsp garlic powder
- 1/2 tsp onion powder
- Salt and pepper, to taste

Instruction:

1. Evenly dividing pork ribs between the two zone. Select Zone 1, choose the AIR FRY program, and set the temperature to 140°C. Set the time to 45 minutes. Select MATCH. Press the START/STOP button to begin air frying the pork ribs.
2. While the ribs are air frying, in a separate bowl, mix together the BBQ sauce, brown sugar, apple cider vinegar, Worcestershire sauce, smoked paprika, garlic powder, onion powder, salt, and pepper to create the BBQ sauce.
3. After 45 minutes of air frying, carefully remove the pork ribs from the air fryer.
4. Brush the ribs with the prepared BBQ sauce, ensuring they are evenly coated.
5. Place the coated ribs back into both zone. Select Zone 1, choose the AIR FRY program, and set the temperature to 140°C. Set the time to an additional 15 minutes. Select MATCH. Press the START/STOP button to continue air frying the BBQ Ribs.
6. While the ribs are air frying, periodically brush them with more BBQ sauce for added flavor and moisture.
7. After the additional 15 minutes of air frying, carefully remove the BBQ Ribs from the air fryer.
8. Allow the ribs to rest for a few minutes before serving. Serve the **BBQ Ribs** with additional BBQ sauce on the side, if desired.

CHAPTER 04: DINNER/SUPPER

BBQ Tilapia

Prep: 10 Min | Cook: 12 Min | Serves: 4

Ingredient:

- 4 tilapia fillets (about 150g each)
- 2 tbsp olive oil
- 2 tbsp BBQ sauce
- 1 tbsp lemon juice
- 1 tsp smoked paprika
- 1/2 tsp garlic powder
- 1/2 tsp onion powder
- Salt and pepper, to taste
- Fresh parsley, chopped (for garnish)

Instruction:

1. In a small bowl, mix together the olive oil, BBQ sauce, lemon juice, smoked paprika, garlic powder, onion powder, salt, and pepper to create the marinade.
2. Place the tilapia fillets in a shallow dish and pour the marinade over them, ensuring they are evenly coated. Let them marinate for about 5 minutes.
3. In Zone 1 of the Ninja Dual Zone Air Fryer, place the marinated tilapia fillets.
4. Select Zone 1, choose the AIR FRY program, and set the temperature to 200°C. Set the time to 10-12 minutes.
5. Press the START/STOP button to begin air frying the BBQ Tilapia.
6. While the tilapia is air frying, periodically baste the fillets with the remaining marinade for added flavor.
7. After 10-12 minutes of air frying, carefully remove the BBQ Tilapia from the air fryer.
8. Garnish with fresh chopped parsley.
9. Serve the **BBQ Tilapia** fillets with your choice of sides, such as steamed vegetables or a salad.

Baked Potatoes

Prep: 5 Min | Cook: 50 Min | Serves: 4

Ingredient:

- 4 medium-sized potatoes
- Olive oil
- Salt and pepper, to taste
- Optional toppings: butter, sour cream, grated cheese, chopped chives

Instruction:

1. Scrub the potatoes clean under running water. Pat them dry with a kitchen towel.
2. Pierce each potato several times with a fork to allow steam to escape during cooking.
3. Rub each potato with olive oil, ensuring they are evenly coated.
4. Sprinkle salt and pepper over the oiled potatoes, to taste.
5. In Zone 1 of the air fryer, place the potatoes. Select Zone 1, choose the AIR FRY program, and set the temperature to 200°C. Set the time to 40-50 minutes, depending on the size of the potatoes. Press the START/STOP button to begin cooking.
6. After 20 minutes of cooking, open the air fryer and flip the potatoes. This will help them cook evenly.
7. Close the air fryer and continue cooking for the remaining time or until the potatoes are tender and cooked through. You can test the doneness by inserting a fork or skewer into the center of a potato. If it goes in easily, they are ready.
8. Once the potatoes are cooked, remove them from the air fryer and allow them to cool slightly.
9. Slice each potato open lengthwise and fluff the insides with a fork.
10. Serve the **Baked Potatoe**s with your choice of toppings, such as butter, sour cream, grated cheese, or chopped chives.

CHAPTER 04: DINNER/SUPPER

Beef and Potato Curry

Prep: 15 Min | Cook: 75 Min | Serves: 4-6

Ingredient:

- 500g beef, cut into cubes
- 2 medium potatoes, peeled and diced
- 1 onion, chopped
- 2 cloves garlic, minced
- 2 tbsp curry paste (such as Madras or Tikka)
- 400ml coconut milk
- 200ml beef stock
- 1 tbsp vegetable oil
- 1 tsp turmeric powder
- Salt and pepper, to taste
- Fresh coriander, chopped (for garnish)

Instruction:

1. In Zone 1, place the beef cubes. Select Zone 1, choose the AIR FRY program, and set the temperature to 180°C. Set the time to 15 minutes. Press the START/STOP.
2. While the beef is air frying, in a separate pan, heat the vegetable oil over medium heat. Add the chopped onion and minced garlic to the pan and sauté until the onion becomes translucent.
3. Add the curry paste and turmeric powder to the pan, stirring well to coat the onions and garlic.
4. Add the diced potatoes to the pan and cook for a few minutes, stirring occasionally.
5. Pour in the coconut milk and beef stock, and season with salt and pepper. Stir to combine all the ingredients.
6. Then cooked beef cubes, add the potato and curry mixture from the pan to Zone 1 as well.
7. Select Zone 1, choose the ROAST program, and set the temperature to 180°C. Set the time to 1 hour. Press the START/STOP button to begin roasting the beef and potato curry.
8. After 1 hour of roasting, carefully remove the beef and potato curry from the air fryer.
9. Garnish with fresh chopped coriander before serving.
10. Serve the **Beef and Potato Curry** with steamed rice or naan bread.

Cajun Shrimp

Prep: 10 Min | Cook: 10 Min | Serves: 4

Ingredient:

- 500g large shrimp, peeled and deveined
- 2 tablespoons olive oil
- 2 teaspoons Cajun seasoning
- 1 teaspoon paprika
- 1/2 teaspoon garlic powder
- 1/2 teaspoon onion powder
- 1/4 teaspoon dried thyme
- 1/4 teaspoon dried oregano
- 1/4 teaspoon salt
- 1/4 teaspoon black pepper
- Lemon wedges, for serving
- Fresh parsley, chopped (optional, for garnish)

Instruction:

1. In a large bowl, add the peeled and deveined shrimp.
2. Drizzle the shrimp with olive oil and toss to coat evenly.
3. In a separate small bowl, combine the Cajun seasoning, paprika, garlic powder, onion powder, dried thyme, dried oregano, salt, and black pepper. Mix well to create the Cajun spice blend.
4. Sprinkle the Cajun spice blend over the shrimp, ensuring they are well coated. Toss to evenly distribute the spices.
5. In Zone 1 of the air fryer, place the seasoned shrimp. Select Zone 1, choose the AIR FRY program, and set the temperature to 200°C. Set the time to 8-10 minutes.
6. Press the START/STOP button to begin cooking.
7. After 4-5 minutes of cooking, open the air fryer and shake the basket or flip the shrimp for even cooking.
8. Close the air fryer and continue cooking for the remaining time or until the shrimp are pink, opaque, and cooked through.
9. Once done, remove the Cajun Shrimp from the air fryer and transfer them to a serving plate.
10. Serve the **Cajun Shrimp** with lemon wedges for squeezing over the shrimp and garnish with fresh chopped parsley, if desired.

CHAPTER 04: DINNER/SUPPER

Cajun Tilapia

Prep: 10 Min | Cook: 10 Min | Serves: 4

Ingredient:

- 4 tilapia fillets (about 150g each)
- 2 tablespoons olive oil
- 1 tablespoon Cajun seasoning
- 1/2 teaspoon paprika
- 1/2 teaspoon garlic powder
- 1/2 teaspoon onion powder
- 1/4 teaspoon dried thyme
- 1/4 teaspoon dried oregano
- 1/4 teaspoon salt
- 1/4 teaspoon black pepper
- Lemon wedges, for serving
- Fresh parsley, chopped (optional, for garnish)

Instruction:

1. In a small bowl, combine the Cajun seasoning, paprika, garlic powder, onion powder, dried thyme, dried oregano, salt, and black pepper. Mix well to create the Cajun spice blend.
2. Brush each tilapia fillet with olive oil on both sides.
3. Sprinkle the Cajun spice blend over the tilapia fillets, ensuring they are well coated on all sides.
4. In Zone 1 of the air fryer, place the seasoned tilapia fillets. Select Zone 1, choose the AIR FRY program, and set the temperature to 200°C. Set the time to 8-10 minutes. Press the START/STOP button to begin cooking.
5. After 4-5 minutes of cooking, open the air fryer and flip the tilapia fillets for even cooking.
6. Close the air fryer and continue cooking for the remaining time or until the tilapia is opaque and flakes easily with a fork.
7. Once done, remove the Cajun Tilapia from the air fryer and transfer them to a serving plate.
8. Serve the **Cajun Tilapia** with lemon wedges for squeezing over the fish and garnish with fresh chopped parsley, if desired.

Chicken and Bacon Potato Skins

Prep: 15 Min | Cook: 55 Min | Serves: 4

Ingredient:

- 4 large baking potatoes
- 200g cooked chicken, shredded or diced
- 100g bacon, cooked and crumbled
- 100g cheddar cheese, grated
- 2 tablespoons sour cream
- 2 tablespoons chopped fresh chives
- Salt and pepper, to taste

Instruction:

1. Scrub the potatoes clean under running water. Pat them dry with a kitchen towel. Pierce each potato several times with a fork to allow steam to escape during cooking.
2. In Zone 1, place the potatoes. Choose the AIR FRY program, and set the temperature to 200°C. Set the time to 40-45 minutes. Press the START/STOP button to begin cooking.
3. After 20 minutes of cooking, open the air fryer and flip the potatoes. This will help them cook evenly. Once the potatoes are cooked, remove them from the air fryer and allow them to cool slightly.
4. Cut the potatoes in half lengthwise. Scoop out the flesh, leaving about a 0,6cm shell.
5. In a bowl, combine the cooked chicken, crumbled bacon, grated cheddar cheese, sour cream, chopped chives, salt, and pepper. Mix well. Fill each potato skin with the chicken and bacon mixture, dividing it evenly among the potato halves.
6. Place the filled potato skins in Zone 1. Select Zone 1, choose the AIR FRY program, and set the temperature to 200°C. Set the time to 8-10 minutes. Press the START/STOP. After 4-5 minutes of cooking, open the air fryer and sprinkle some additional grated cheese on top of each potato skin.
7. Once done, remove the **Chicken and Bacon Potato Skins** from the air fryer and transfer them to a serving plate. Serve the potato skins hot, garnished with additional chopped chives if desired.

CHAPTER 04: DINNER/SUPPER

Chicken and Mushroom Gnocchi

Prep: 10 Min | Cook: 20 Min | Serves: 4

Ingredient:

- 500g gnocchi
- 2 chicken breasts, diced
- 200g mushrooms, sliced
- 1 onion, finely chopped
- 2 cloves garlic, minced
- 200ml double cream
- 100g grated Parmesan cheese
- 2 tablespoons olive oil
- 1 tablespoon butter
- 1 teaspoon dried thyme
- Salt and pepper, to taste
- Fresh parsley, chopped (for garnish)

Instruction:

1. In a large frying pan, heat the olive oil and butter over medium heat. Add the chopped onions to the pan and cook until they become translucent, about 3-4 minutes. Add the minced garlic and sliced mushrooms to the pan. Cook for another 5 minutes or until the mushrooms have softened and released their moisture.
2. Add the diced chicken to the pan and cook until it is browned and cooked through, about 8-10 minutes.
3. Meanwhile, in Zone 1, place the gnocchi. Select Zone 1, choose the AIR FRY program, and set the temperature to 200°C. Set the time to 8 minutes. Press the START/STOP.
4. While gnocchi cooks, add double cream and dried thyme to the pan with chicken and mushrooms. Season with salt and pepper. Simmer sauce for 2-3 minutes until slightly thickened.
5. Once gnocchi is done, transfer it to the pan with chicken, mushrooms, and cream sauce. Stir gently, sprinkle grated Parmesan cheese, and stir until melted and well combined.
6. In Zone 1, place an oven-safe dish. Transfer the chicken and mushroom gnocchi mixture to the dish. Select Zone 1, choose the AIR FRY program, and set the temperature to 200°C. Set the time to 8-10 minutes. Press the START/STOP. After 4-5 minutes of cooking, open the air fryer and check if the gnocchi is heated through and the top is slightly browned.
7. Once done, remove the **Chicken and Mushroom Gnocchi** from the air fryer and garnish with freshly chopped parsley.

Chicken and Vegetable Frittata

Prep: 15 Min | Cook: 20 Min | Serves: 4

Ingredient:

- 6 large eggs
- 200g cooked chicken, diced
- 100g cherry tomatoes, halved
- 100g baby spinach
- 1/2 red bell pepper, diced
- 1/2 red onion, diced
- 50g grated cheddar cheese
- 2 tablespoons olive oil
- 1 tablespoon chopped fresh parsley
- Salt and pepper, to taste

Instruction:

1. Heat the olive oil in a frying pan over medium heat.
2. Add the diced red bell pepper and red onion to the pan. Sauté for 3-4 minutes until they become slightly softened.
3. Add the baby spinach to the pan and cook until it wilts, about 2 minutes.
4. In a bowl, whisk the eggs until well beaten. Season with salt and pepper.
5. Add the cooked chicken, halved cherry tomatoes, grated cheddar cheese, and chopped parsley to the bowl with the beaten eggs. Mix well to combine.
6. In Zone 1 of the air fryer, place an oven-safe dish. Pour the egg mixture into the dish. Select Zone 1, choose the AIR FRY program, and set the temperature to 180°C. Set the time to 15-20 minutes.
7. Press the START/STOP button to begin cooking.
8. After 8-10 minutes of cooking, open the air fryer and gently stir the frittata mixture to ensure even cooking.
9. Close the air fryer and continue cooking for the remaining time or until the frittata is set in the center and the top is golden brown.
10. Once done, remove the **Chicken and Vegetable Frittata** from the air fryer and allow it to cool slightly.
11. Cut the frittata into slices and serve warm.

CHAPTER 03: LUNCH

Cornish Pasties

Prep: 30 Min | Cook: 30 Min | Serves: 4

Ingredient:

For the Pastry:
- 500g plain flour
- 225g unsalted butter, cold and diced
- 1 teaspoon salt
- 120ml cold water

For the Filling:
- 400g beef skirt or chuck steak, diced
- 200g potato, peeled and diced
- 100g swede (rutabaga), peeled and diced
- 100g onion, finely chopped
- Salt and pepper, to taste
- 1 egg, beaten (for egg wash)

Instruction:

1. In a large mixing bowl, combine the flour, salt, and diced cold butter. Rub the mixture together with your fingertips until it resembles breadcrumbs. Gradually add the cold water to the mixture, a little at a time, and mix until the dough comes together. Use your hands to bring the dough into a ball.
2. On a lightly floured surface, roll out the pastry dough to a thickness of about 3-4mm.
3. Using a plate or a round cutter about 20cm in diameter, cut out four circles from the pastry dough.
4. In a separate bowl, combine the diced beef, potato, swede, and chopped onion. Season with salt and pepper to taste.
5. Place a portion of the filling mixture onto one half of each pastry circle, leaving a small border around the edge.
6. Fold the pastry over the filling to form a half-moon shape. Press the edges firmly together to seal, and crimp the edges with your fingers or a fork.
7. Evenly dividing pasties between the two zone. Select Zone 1, choose the AIR FRY program, and set temperature to 200°C. Set time to 25-30 minutes. Select MATCH. Press the START/STOP.
8. After 15-20 minutes of cooking, open the air fryer and brush the pasties with beaten egg wash. This will give them a golden brown color. Once done, remove the **Cornish Pasties** from the air fryer and allow them to cool slightly before serving.

Garlic Butter Steak

Prep: 10 Min | Cook: 12 Min | Serves: 4

Ingredient:

- 2 ribeye steaks (approximately 250g each)
- 4 tablespoons unsalted butter, softened
- 4 garlic cloves, minced
- 1 teaspoon chopped fresh parsley
- Salt and pepper, to taste

➤ Instruction:

1. In a small bowl, combine the softened butter, minced garlic, chopped parsley, salt, and pepper. Mix well to make the garlic butter.
2. Season both sides of the ribeye steaks with salt and pepper.
3. Evenly dividing steak between the two zone. Select Zone 1, choose the AIR FRY program, and set the temperature to 200°C. Set the time to 10-12 minutes. Select MATCH. Press the START/STOP button to begin cooking.
4. After 5-6 minutes of cooking, open the air fryer and carefully flip the steaks using tongs.
5. Close the air fryer and continue cooking for the remaining time or until the steaks reach your desired level of doneness. For medium-rare, cook for about 10 minutes. Adjust the cooking time based on your preference.
6. Once the steaks are cooked to your liking, carefully remove them from the air fryer and transfer them to a plate.
7. While the steaks are still hot, top each steak with a generous dollop of garlic butter. Allow the butter to melt and coat the steaks.
8. Let the steaks rest for a few minutes to allow the flavors to meld together. Serve the **Garlic Butter Steak** with your choice of sides, such as roasted potatoes or steamed vegetables.

CHAPTER 04: DINNER/SUPPER

Hamburgers

Prep: 10 Min | Cook: 12 Min | Serves: 4

Ingredient:

- 500g ground beef
- 1 small onion, finely chopped
- 1 garlic clove, minced
- 1 teaspoon Worcestershire sauce
- 1 teaspoon Dijon mustard
- 1 teaspoon salt
- 1/2 teaspoon black pepper
- 4 burger buns
- Burger toppings of your choice (lettuce, tomato, cheese, etc.)
- Condiments of your choice (ketchup, mayonnaise, etc.)

➤ Instruction:

1. In a large mixing bowl, combine the ground beef, chopped onion, minced garlic, Worcestershire sauce, Dijon mustard, salt, and black pepper. Mix well until all the ingredients are evenly incorporated.
2. Divide the meat mixture into four equal portions. Shape each portion into a patty about 2cm thick.
3. Evenly dividing burger patties between the two zone. Select Zone 1, choose the AIR FRY program, and set the temperature to 200°C. Set the time to 10-12 minutes. Select MATCH to duplicate settings across both zones. Press the START/STOP button to begin cooking.
4. After 5-6 minutes of cooking, open the air fryer and carefully flip the burger patties using tongs.
5. Close the air fryer and continue cooking for the remaining time or until the burgers reach your desired level of doneness.
6. Once done, remove the burger patties from the air fryer and let them rest for a few minutes.
7. While the patties are resting, lightly toast the burger buns in the air fryer for 1-2 minutes, if desired.
8. Assemble your hamburgers by placing a cooked patty on the bottom half of each bun. Add your desired toppings and condiments.
9. Serve the **hamburgers** immediately and enjoy!

Honey Mustard Salmon

Prep: 10 Min | Cook: 12 Min | Serves: 2

Ingredient:

- 2 salmon fillets (approximately 150g each)
- 2 tablespoons honey
- 2 tablespoons Dijon mustard
- 1 tablespoon olive oil
- 1 tablespoon lemon juice
- Salt and pepper, to taste
- Fresh dill or parsley, for garnish (optional)

Instruction:

1. In a small bowl, whisk together the honey, Dijon mustard, olive oil, lemon juice, salt, and pepper to make the honey mustard glaze.
2. Place the salmon fillets in a shallow dish and pour the honey mustard glaze over them. Use a spoon or brush to coat the salmon evenly with the glaze.
3. Place two salmon fillet in two zone. Select Zone 1, choose the AIR FRY program, and set the temperature to 200°C. Set the time to 10-12 minutes. Select MATCH to duplicate settings across both zones. Press the START/STOP button to begin cooking.
4. After 5-6 minutes of cooking, open the air fryer and carefully flip the salmon fillets using a spatula.
5. Close the air fryer and continue cooking for the remaining time or until the salmon is cooked through and flakes easily with a fork.
6. Once the salmon is cooked, carefully remove the fillets from the air fryer and transfer them to a serving plate.
7. Garnish with fresh dill or parsley, if desired.
8. Serve the **Honey Mustard Salmon** with your choice of sides, such as steamed vegetables or a salad.

CHAPTER 04: DINNER/SUPPER

Kedgeree

Prep: 10 Min | Cook: 20 Min | Serves: 2

Ingredient:

- 200g smoked haddock fillets
- 200g basmati rice
- 2 large eggs
- 1 medium onion, finely chopped
- 2 cloves of garlic, minced
- 1 teaspoon curry powder
- 1/2 teaspoon turmeric powder
- 1/2 teaspoon cumin powder
- 1/2 teaspoon coriander powder
- 1 tablespoon vegetable oil
- 1 lemon, juiced
- Fresh cilantro (coriander), chopped, for garnish
- Salt and pepper, to taste

Instruction:

1. In Zone 1, place the smoked haddock fillets. Select Zone 1, choose the AIR FRY program, and set the temperature to 180°C. Set the time to 10 minutes. Press the START/STOP.
2. While the haddock is cooking, in a separate pot, cook the basmati rice according to the package instructions. Once cooked, fluff the rice with a fork and set it aside.
3. In Zone 1, place the eggs. Select Zone 1, choose the AIR FRY program, and set the temperature to 180°C. Set the time to 10 minutes for hard-boiled eggs. Press the START/STOP.
4. In a large frying pan or skillet, heat the vegetable oil over medium heat. Add the chopped onion and minced garlic, and sauté until the onion becomes translucent. Add the curry powder, turmeric powder, cumin powder, and coriander powder to the pan. Stir well to coat the onions and garlic with the spices.
5. Flake the cooked haddock into the pan, discarding any skin or bones. Stir gently to combine the fish with the spices.
6. Add the cooked basmati rice to the pan and stir to mix everything together. Season with salt and pepper to taste.
7. Once the eggs are done cooking in the air fryer, let them cool slightly. Peel the eggs and chop them into small pieces. Add it to the pan and gently mix them into the rice and fish mixture.
8. Squeeze the juice of one lemon over the **kedgeree** and stir well to combine all the flavors. Transfer the kedgeree to serving plates or bowls and garnish with fresh cilantro.

Liver and Onions

Prep: 15 Min | Cook: 25 Min | Serves: 4

Ingredient:

- 500g lamb or beef liver, sliced
- 2 large onions, thinly sliced
- 2 tbsp vegetable oil
- 2 tbsp butter
- 2 tbsp plain flour
- 200ml beef or vegetable stock
- 1 tsp Worcestershire sauce
- Salt and pepper, to taste
- Fresh parsley, chopped (for garnish)

➤ Instruction:

1. In Zone 1, place the liver slices. Select Zone 1, choose the AIR FRY program, and set the temperature to 200°C. Set the time to 10 minutes. Press the START/STOP.
2. While the liver is air frying, in a separate pan, heat the vegetable oil and butter over medium heat.
3. Add the thinly sliced onions to the pan and cook until they become soft and translucent.
4. Sprinkle the flour over the onions and stir well to coat.
5. Gradually pour in the beef or vegetable stock, stirring constantly to create a thick gravy.
6. Stir in the Worcestershire sauce, salt, and pepper. Remove from heat.
7. After cooked liver slices, pour the prepared onion and gravy mixture from the pan over the liver slices. Select Zone 1, choose the BAKE program, and set the temperature to 180°C. Set the time to 15 minutes.
8. Press the START/STOP button to begin baking the Liver and Onions.
9. After 15 minutes of baking, carefully remove the Liver and Onions from the air fryer. Garnish with fresh chopped parsley before serving. Serve the **Liver and Onions** with mashed potatoes or crusty bread.

CHAPTER 04: DINNER/SUPPER

Lamb and Apricot Tagine

Prep: 20 Min | Cook: 75 Min | Serves: 4-6

Ingredient:

- 500g lamb shoulder, diced
- 2 onions, chopped
- 2 cloves garlic, minced
- 2 carrots, peeled and sliced
- 200g dried apricots
- 400g canned chopped tomatoes
- 400ml lamb or vegetable stock
- 2 tbsp olive oil
- 2 tsp ground cumin
- 2 tsp ground coriander
- 1 tsp ground cinnamon
- 1 tsp turmeric
- Salt and pepper, to taste
- Fresh coriander, chopped (for garnish)

➤ Instruction:

1. In Zone 1, place the diced lamb shoulder. Select Zone 1, choose the AIR FRY program, and set the temperature to 180°C. Set the time to 15 minutes. Press the START/STOP button to begin air frying the lamb shoulder. This will help sear and brown the meat.
2. While the lamb is air frying, in a separate pan, heat the olive oil over medium heat.
3. Add the chopped onions and minced garlic to the pan and sauté until the onions become translucent.
4. Add the ground cumin, ground coriander, ground cinnamon, and turmeric to the pan, stirring well to coat the onions and garlic.
5. Add the sliced carrots, dried apricots, canned chopped tomatoes, and lamb or vegetable stock to the pan. Stir to combine all the ingredients.
6. After cooked lamb shoulder, pour the prepared mixture from the pan over the lamb shoulde. Select Zone 1, choose the ROAST program, and set the temperature to 180°C. Set the time to 1 hour. Press the START/STOP.
7. After 1 hour of roasting, carefully remove the Lamb and Apricot Tagine from the air fryer.
8. Season with salt and pepper, to taste. Garnish with fresh chopped coriander before serving.
9. Serve the **Lamb and Apricot Tagine** with couscous or rice.

Lamb and Vegetable Stir-Fry

Prep: 15 Min | Cook: 15 Min | Serves: 4

Ingredient:

- 400g boneless lamb leg, thinly sliced
- 2 tablespoons soy sauce
- 2 tablespoons oyster sauce
- 1 tablespoon cornstarch
- 2 tablespoons vegetable oil
- 2 cloves of garlic, minced
- 1 red bell pepper, thinly sliced
- 1 yellow bell pepper, thinly sliced
- 1 medium carrot, julienned
- 150g sugar snap peas
- 1 medium onion, thinly sliced
- Salt and pepper, to taste
- Fresh cilantro (coriander), chopped, for garnish (optional)

Instruction:

1. In a bowl, combine the sliced lamb, soy sauce, oyster sauce, and cornstarch. Mix well and let it marinate for 10 minutes.
2. In Zone 1 of the air fryer, place the marinated lamb slices. Select Zone 1, choose the AIR FRY program, and set the temperature to 200°C. Set the time to 8 minutes.
3. Press the START/STOP button to begin cooking.
4. In a large frying pan or skillet, heat the vegetable oil over medium heat. Add the minced garlic and sauté until fragrant.
5. Add the sliced bell peppers, julienned carrot, sugar snap peas, and sliced onion to the pan. Stir-fry for about 5 minutes until the vegetables are tender-crisp.
6. Once the lamb is done cooking in the air fryer, add it to the pan with the stir-fried vegetables. Stir well to combine.
7. Season the stir-fry with salt and pepper to taste. Adjust the seasoning according to your preference.
8. In Zone 1 of the air fryer, transfer the lamb and vegetable stir-fry. Select Zone 1, choose the AIR FRY program, and set the temperature to 200°C. Set the time to 7 minutes.
9. Press the START/STOP button to begin cooking.
10. Once cooked, remove the **lamb and vegetable stir-fry** from the air fryer and let it cool slightly.
11. Serve the stir-fry hot, garnished with fresh cilantro if desired.

CHAPTER 04: DINNER/SUPPER

Mac and Cheese

Prep: 10 Min | Cook: 20 Min | Serves: 4

Ingredient:

- 250g macaroni pasta
- 250g cheddar cheese, grated
- 50g butter
- 50g all-purpose flour
- 500ml milk
- 1 teaspoon Dijon mustard
- Salt and pepper, to taste
- Breadcrumbs, for topping (optional)
- Fresh parsley, chopped, for garnish (optional)

Instruction:

1. In Zone 1, place the macaroni pasta. Select Zone 1, choose the AIR FRY program, and set the temperature to 180°C. Set the time to 10 minutes. Press the START/STOP.
2. While the pasta is cooking, in a separate saucepan, melt the butter over medium heat.
3. Add the flour to the melted butter and whisk continuously for about 1 minute to form a roux.
4. Gradually pour in the milk while whisking constantly to create a smooth sauce. Continue whisking until the sauce thickens.
5. Stir in the grated cheddar cheese and Dijon mustard until the cheese is fully melted and the sauce is smooth. Season with salt and pepper to taste.
6. Once the pasta is done cooking in the air fryer, drain it and add it to the cheese sauce. Stir well to coat the pasta evenly.
7. In Zone 1, transfer the mac and cheese mixture. Select Zone 1, choose the AIR FRY program, and set the temperature to 180°C. Set the time to 10 minutes. Press the START/STOP.
8. If desired, sprinkle breadcrumbs over the top of the mac and cheese for a crispy crust. Return the dish to the air fryer and continue cooking until the top is golden and crispy.
9. Once cooked, remove the Mac and Cheese from the air fryer and let it cool slightly. Serve the **Mac and Cheese** hot, garnished with fresh parsley if desired.

Maple Glazed Salmon

Prep: 10 Min | Cook: 10 Min | Serves: 4

Ingredient:

- 4 salmon fillets (about 150g each)
- 4 tablespoons maple syrup
- 2 tablespoons soy sauce
- 1 tablespoon Dijon mustard
- 1 tablespoon lemon juice
- 1 tablespoon vegetable oil
- Salt and pepper, to taste
- Fresh parsley, chopped, for garnish (optional)

▶ Instruction:

1. In a small bowl, whisk together the maple syrup, soy sauce, Dijon mustard, lemon juice, vegetable oil, salt, and pepper to make the glaze.
2. In Zone 1 of the air fryer, place the salmon fillets. Select Zone 1, choose the AIR FRY program, and set the temperature to 180°C. Set the time to 4 minutes.
3. Press the START/STOP button to begin cooking.
4. After 4 minutes, open the air fryer and brush each salmon fillet with the maple glaze.
5. Close the air fryer and continue cooking for another 4 minutes or until the salmon is cooked to your desired level of doneness.
6. In Zone 2 of the air fryer, transfer the remaining maple glaze. Select Zone 2, choose the AIR FRY program, and set the temperature to 180°C. Set the time to 3 minutes.
7. Press the START/STOP button to begin cooking.
8. Once the glaze has thickened slightly, remove it from the air fryer.
9. Remove the cooked salmon fillets from the air fryer and let them rest for a minute.
10. Drizzle the thickened maple glaze over the salmon fillets.
11. Serve the **Maple Glazed Salmon** hot, garnished with fresh parsley if desired.

CHAPTER 04: DINNER/SUPPER

Maple Glazed Tilapia

Prep: 10 Min | Cook: 10 Min | Serves: 4

Ingredient:

- 4 tilapia fillets (about 150g each)
- 2 tablespoons maple syrup
- 1 tablespoon soy sauce
- 1 tablespoon Dijon mustard
- 1 tablespoon lemon juice
- 1 tablespoon vegetable oil
- Salt and pepper, to taste
- Fresh parsley, chopped, for garnish (optional)

▶ Instruction:

1. In a small bowl, whisk together the maple syrup, soy sauce, Dijon mustard, lemon juice, vegetable oil, salt, and pepper to make the glaze.
2. In Zone 1 of the air fryer, place the tilapia fillets. Select Zone 1, choose the AIR FRY program, and set the temperature to 180°C. Set the time to 4 minutes.
3. Press the START/STOP button to begin cooking.
4. After 4 minutes, open the air fryer and brush each tilapia fillet with the maple glaze.
5. Close the air fryer and continue cooking for another 4 minutes or until the tilapia is cooked through and flakes easily with a fork.
6. In Zone 2 of the air fryer, transfer the remaining maple glaze. Select Zone 2, choose the AIR FRY program, and set the temperature to 180°C. Set the time to 3 minutes.
7. Press the START/STOP button to begin cooking.
8. Once the glaze has thickened slightly, remove it from the air fryer.
9. Remove the cooked tilapia fillets from the air fryer and let them rest for a minute.
10. Drizzle the thickened maple glaze over the tilapia fillets.
11. Serve the **Maple Glazed Tilapia** hot, garnished with fresh parsley if desired.

Orange Glazed Pork Chops

Prep: 15 Min | Cook: 15 Min | Serves: 4

Ingredient:

- 4 pork chops (about 200g each)
- Zest and juice of 1 orange
- 2 tablespoons honey
- 2 tablespoons soy sauce
- 1 tablespoon vegetable oil
- 1 teaspoon Dijon mustard
- 2 cloves of garlic, minced
- Salt and pepper, to taste
- Fresh parsley, chopped, for garnish (optional)

▶ Instruction:

1. In a small bowl, combine the orange zest, orange juice, honey, soy sauce, vegetable oil, Dijon mustard, minced garlic, salt, and pepper to make the glaze.
2. In Zone 1 of the air fryer, place the pork chops. Select Zone 1, choose the AIR FRY program, and set the temperature to 200°C. Set the time to 8 minutes. Press the START/STOP button to begin cooking.
3. After 8 minutes, open the air fryer and brush each pork chop with the orange glaze.
4. Close the air fryer and continue cooking for another 6-7 minutes or until the pork chops are cooked through and reach an internal temperature of 63°C.
5. In Zone 2 of the air fryer, transfer the remaining orange glaze. Select Zone 2, choose the AIR FRY program, and set the temperature to 180°C. Set the time to 3 minutes.
6. Press the START/STOP button to begin cooking.
7. Once the glaze has thickened slightly, remove it from the air fryer.
8. Remove the cooked pork chops from the air fryer and let them rest for a few minutes. Drizzle the thickened orange glaze over the pork chops. Serve the **Orange Glazed Pork Chops** hot, garnished with fresh parsley if desired.

CHAPTER 04: DINNER/SUPPER

Orange Glazed Salmon

Prep: 15 Min | Cook: 10 Min | Serves: 4

Ingredient:

- 4 salmon fillets (about 150g each)
- Zest and juice of 1 orange
- 2 tablespoons honey
- 2 tablespoons soy sauce
- 1 tablespoon vegetable oil
- 1 teaspoon Dijon mustard
- 2 cloves of garlic, minced
- Salt and pepper, to taste
- Fresh parsley, chopped, for garnish (optional)

▶ Instruction:

1. In a small bowl, combine the orange zest, orange juice, honey, soy sauce, vegetable oil, Dijon mustard, minced garlic, salt, and pepper to make the glaze.
2. In Zone 1 of the air fryer, place the salmon fillets. Select Zone 1, choose the AIR FRY program, and set the temperature to 180°C. Set the time to 4 minutes.
3. Press the START/STOP button to begin cooking.
4. After 4 minutes, open the air fryer and brush each salmon fillet with the orange glaze.
5. Close the air fryer and continue cooking for another 4-5 minutes or until the salmon is cooked through and flakes easily with a fork.
6. In Zone 2 of the air fryer, transfer the remaining orange glaze. Select Zone 2, choose the AIR FRY program, and set the temperature to 180°C. Set the time to 3 minutes.
7. Press the START/STOP button to begin cooking.
8. Once the glaze has thickened slightly, remove it from the air fryer.
9. Remove the cooked salmon fillets from the air fryer and let them rest for a few minutes.
10. Drizzle the thickened orange glaze over the salmon fillets.
11. Serve the **Orange Glazed Salmon** hot, garnished with fresh parsley if desired.

Pasties

Prep: 30 Min | Cook: 12 Min | Serves: 4

Ingredient:

For the pastry:
- 300g plain flour
- 150g cold unsalted butter, diced
- 1/2 teaspoon salt
- 6-8 tablespoons cold water

For the filling:
- 300g beef steak, diced
- 1 onion, finely chopped
- 2 potatoes, peeled and diced
- 150g swede (rutabaga), peeled and diced
- Salt and pepper, to taste
- 1 tablespoon Worcestershire sauce

Instruction:

1. In a large bowl, combine the plain flour, cold unsalted butter, and salt. Use your fingertips to rub the butter into the flour until the mixture resembles breadcrumbs.
2. Gradually add the cold water, 1 tablespoon at a time, and mix until the dough comes together. Gather the dough into a ball, wrap it in plastic wrap, and refrigerate for 15 minutes.
3. In the meantime, prepare the filling. In a bowl, mix together the beef steak, chopped onion, diced potatoes, diced swede, salt, pepper, and Worcestershire sauce.
4. On a floured surface, roll out the pastry to a thickness of about 3-4mm. Cut out four circles, approximately 20cm in diameter.
5. Divide the filling equally among the pastry circles, placing it on one side of each circle, leaving a border around the edge.
6. Fold the other half of each pastry circle over the filling to form a semicircle. Press the edges together firmly to seal.
7. Evenly dividing pasties between the two zone. Select Zone 1, choose the AIR FRY program, and set the temperature to 180°C. Set the time to 12 minutes. Select MATCH. Press the START/STOP button to begin cooking.
8. After 12 minutes, swap the pasties between the two zones to ensure even cooking. Continue cooking for another 12-13 minutes or until the pasties are golden brown and cooked through. Enjoy your delicious homemade **Pasties**!

CHAPTER 04: DINNER/SUPPER

Salmon with Lemon and Herbs

Prep: 10 Min | Cook: 10 Min | Serves: 4

Ingredient:

- 4 salmon fillets (about 150g each)
- Zest and juice of 1 lemon
- 2 tablespoons olive oil
- 2 cloves of garlic, minced
- 1 tablespoon fresh dill, chopped
- 1 tablespoon fresh parsley, chopped
- Salt and pepper, to taste
- Lemon slices, for garnish (optional)

Instruction:

1. In a small bowl, combine the lemon zest, lemon juice, olive oil, minced garlic, chopped dill, chopped parsley, salt, and pepper to make the marinade.
2. Place the salmon fillets in a shallow dish and pour the marinade over them. Let the salmon marinate for about 10 minutes.
3. In Zone 1 of the air fryer, place the salmon fillets. Select Zone 1, choose the AIR FRY program, and set the temperature to 200°C. Set the time to 10 minutes.
4. Press the START/STOP button to begin cooking.
5. After 5 minutes, open the air fryer and brush each salmon fillet with the remaining marinade.
6. Close the air fryer and continue cooking for another 4-5 minutes or until the salmon is cooked through and flakes easily with a fork.
7. Remove the cooked salmon fillets from the air fryer and let them rest for a few minutes.
8. Serve the **Salmon with Lemon and Herbs** hot, garnished with warmed lemon slices if desired.

Scampi and Chips

Prep: 15 Min | Cook: 30 Min | Serves: 4

Ingredient:

For the scampi:
- 500g raw scampi
- 100g plain flour
- 2 eggs, beaten
- 100g breadcrumbs
- 1 teaspoon paprika
- Salt and pepper, to taste

For the chips:
- 4 large potatoes, cut into chips
- 2 tablespoons vegetable oil
- Salt, to taste

For serving:
- Lemon wedges
- Tartare sauce

Instruction:

1. In a shallow bowl or dish, combine the plain flour with salt and pepper. In a separate bowl, beat the eggs. In another bowl, mix together the breadcrumbs and paprika.
2. Dip each scampi into the flour mixture, then into the beaten eggs, and finally into the breadcrumb mixture, ensuring they are coated evenly. Place the coated scampi on a plate or tray.
3. In Zone 1 of the air fryer, place the scampi. Select Zone 1, choose the AIR FRY program, and set the temperature to 200°C. Set the time to 8 minutes. Press the START/STOP.
4. In Zone 2, place the cut potatoes for the chips. Drizzle them with vegetable oil and toss to coat evenly. Select Zone 2, choose the AIR FRY program, and set the temperature to 200°C. Set the time to 20 minutes. Press the START/STOP.
5. After 8 minutes, open the air fryer and carefully flip the scampi using tongs or a spatula. Close the air fryer and continue cooking for another 5-6 minutes or until the scampi are golden brown and cooked through.
6. Once the chips are cooked, remove them from the air fryer and sprinkle with salt.
7. Remove the cooked scampi from the air fryer and let them drain on a paper towel. Serve the **Scampi and Chips** hot, accompanied by lemon wedges and tartare sauce.

CHAPTER 04: DINNER/SUPPER

Salmon en Croute

Prep: 20 Min | Cook: 25 Min | Serves: 4

Ingredient:

- 500g salmon fillet, skinless
- 300g puff pastry, thawed if frozen
- 100g cream cheese
- 2 tablespoons chopped fresh dill
- 1 tablespoon Dijon mustard
- Salt and pepper, to taste
- 1 egg, beaten (for egg wash)

Instruction:

1. In a small bowl, combine the cream cheese, chopped fresh dill, Dijon mustard, salt, and pepper. Mix well to create the filling.
2. On a lightly floured surface, roll out the puff pastry to a rectangle large enough to wrap around the salmon fillet.
3. In Zone 1 of the air fryer, place the rolled-out puff pastry. Select Zone 1, choose the AIR FRY program, and set the temperature to 200°C. Set the time to 3 minutes. Press the START/STOP.
4. After 3 minutes, open the air fryer and carefully remove the partially cooked puff pastry from Zone 1. Set it aside.
5. In Zone 1 of the air fryer, place the salmon fillet. Select Zone 1, choose the AIR FRY program, and set the temperature to 200°C. Set the time to 5 minutes. Press the START/STOP.
6. While the salmon is cooking, spread the cream cheese mixture evenly over the puff pastry rectangle.
7. Once the salmon is cooked, remove it from the air fryer and place it on top of the cream cheese mixture on the puff pastry.
8. Fold the edges of the puff pastry over the salmon, sealing it completely. Trim off any excess pastry if necessary.
9. Brush the puff pastry with beaten egg for a golden finish.
10. In Zone1 , place the salmon en croute. Select Zone 1, choose the AIR FRY program, and set the temperature to 200°C. Set the time to 20 minutes. After 20 minutes, or until the puff pastry is golden brown and crisp. Enjoy your delicious **Salmon en Croute**!

Teriyaki Tilapia

Prep: 10 Min | Cook: 10 Min | Serves: 4

Ingredient:

- 4 tilapia fillets
- 4 tablespoons teriyaki sauce
- 2 tablespoons soy sauce
- 2 tablespoons honey
- 1 tablespoon rice vinegar
- 1 teaspoon grated ginger
- 1 clove garlic, minced
- 1 tablespoon vegetable oil
- Sesame seeds, for garnish (optional)
- Sliced spring onions, for garnish (optional)

Instruction:

1. In a small bowl, whisk together the teriyaki sauce, soy sauce, honey, rice vinegar, grated ginger, and minced garlic.
2. In Zone 1 of the air fryer, place the tilapia fillets. Select Zone 1, choose the AIR FRY program, and set the temperature to 200°C. Set the time to 5 minutes.
3. Press the START/STOP button to begin cooking.
4. After 5 minutes, open the air fryer and carefully flip the tilapia fillets using tongs or a spatula. Brush the cooked side of the fillets with the teriyaki sauce mixture.
5. Close the air fryer and continue cooking for another 3-5 minutes, or until the tilapia is cooked through and flakes easily with a fork.
6. In Zone 2 of the air fryer, heat the vegetable oil. Select Zone 2, choose the AIR FRY program, and set the temperature to 200°C. Set the time to 2 minutes. Once the oil is hot, add the remaining teriyaki sauce mixture to Zone 2 and cook for 1-2 minutes, stirring continuously, until the sauce thickens slightly.
7. Remove the cooked tilapia fillets from the air fryer and place them on a serving plate.
8. Drizzle the thickened **teriyaki** sauce over the tilapia fillets.
9. Garnish with sesame seeds and sliced spring onions, if desired.

CHAPTER 04: DINNER/SUPPER

Tofu Scramble

Prep: 10 Min | Cook: 15 Min | Serves: 2-3

Ingredient:

- 400g firm tofu, drained and crumbled
- 1 tablespoon vegetable oil
- 1 small onion, chopped
- 1 bell pepper, diced
- 2 cloves garlic, minced
- 1 teaspoon ground turmeric
- 1/2 teaspoon ground cumin
- 1/2 teaspoon ground paprika
- Salt and pepper, to taste
- Fresh parsley or chives, chopped (for garnish)

Instruction:

1. In Zone 1, place the crumbled tofu. Select Zone 1, choose the AIR FRY program, and set the temperature to 180°C. Set the time to 10 minutes. Press the START/STOP.
2. While the tofu is air frying, in a separate pan, heat the vegetable oil over medium heat.
3. Add the chopped onion, bell pepper, and minced garlic to the pan. Sauté until the vegetables become tender.
4. In a small bowl, mix together the nutritional yeast, turmeric, ground cumin, paprika, salt, and pepper.
5. Once the tofu has finished air frying in Zone 1, transfer it to Zone 2 of the air fryer.
6. Sprinkle the prepared spice mixture from the bowl over the tofu in Zone 2.
7. Add the sautéed vegetables from the pan to Zone 2 with the tofu.
8. Select Zone 2, choose the BAKE program, and set the temperature to 180°C. Set the time to 5 minutes.
9. Press the START/STOP button to begin baking the Tofu Scramble.
10. After 5 minutes of baking, carefully remove the Tofu Scramble from the air fryer.
11. Garnish with fresh chopped parsley or chives before serving.
12. Serve the **Tofu Scramble** with toast or as a filling for wraps.

Page 50

Vegetable Quesadillas

Prep: 15 Min | Cook: 10 Min | Serves: 2

Ingredient:

- 1 tablespoon vegetable oil
- 1 small onion, thinly sliced
- 1 red bell pepper, thinly sliced
- 1 small courgette (zucchini), thinly sliced
- 100g mushrooms, sliced
- 1 teaspoon ground cumin
- 1 teaspoon paprika
- Salt and pepper, to taste
- 4 medium-sized tortilla wraps
- 150g grated cheddar cheese
- Optional toppings: salsa, sour cream, guacamole

Instruction:

1. In a frying pan, heat the vegetable oil over medium heat.
2. Add the sliced onion, bell pepper, courgette, and mushrooms to the pan. Sauté for 5-6 minutes until the vegetables are slightly tender.
3. Sprinkle the ground cumin, paprika, salt, and pepper over the vegetables. Stir well to coat the vegetables with the spices. Remove the pan from heat and set aside.
4. Place two tortilla wraps on Zone 1 of the air fryer basket.
5. Select Zone 1 and choose the AIR FRY program. Set the temperature to 180°C and the time to 2 minutes to warm the tortillas. Press the START/STOP to begin warming the tortillas.
6. Once the tortillas are warmed, spread an even layer of grated cheddar cheese over each tortilla on Zone 1.
7. Spoon the sautéed vegetable mixture evenly over the cheese layer on each tortilla.
8. Top with another layer of grated cheddar cheese.
9. Place Zone 1 in the air fryer and select Zone 1, choose the AIR FRY program. Set the temperature to 200°C and the time to 8 minutes. Press the START/STOP.
10. Cut each quesadilla into quarters or desired shape.
11. Serve the **Vegetable Quesadillas** hot, accompanied by salsa, sour cream, guacamole, or any other desired toppings.

CHAPTER 04: DINNER/SUPPER

Welsh Rarebit

Prep: 10 Min | Cook: 5 Min | Serves: 4

Ingredient:

- 50g unsalted butter
- 50g all-purpose flour
- 200ml milk
- 200g grated cheddar cheese
- 1 tablespoon Worcestershire sauce
- 1 teaspoon Dijon mustard
- 4 slices of bread
- Optional toppings: sliced tomato, cooked bacon

Instruction:

1. In a saucepan, melt the butter over medium heat. Add the flour to the melted butter and whisk continuously for 1-2 minutes to form a smooth paste (roux).
2. Gradually pour in the milk while whisking continuously to create a thick sauce.
3. Add the grated cheddar cheese to the sauce and stir until melted and well combined.
4. Stir in the Worcestershire sauce and Dijon mustard. Remove the saucepan from heat and set aside.
5. Place the bread slices on Zone 1 of the air fryer basket.
6. Select Zone 1 and choose the AIR FRY program. Set the temperature to 180°C and the time to 2 minutes to lightly toast the bread. Press the START/STOP.
7. Once the bread is toasted, spread a generous amount of the cheese sauce mixture over each slice of toasted bread.
8. If desired, add sliced tomato or cooked bacon as optional toppings.
9. Place bread slices on Zone 1 in the air fryer. Select Zone 1 and choose the AIR FRY program. Set the temperature to 200°C and the time to 3 minutes. Press the START/STOP.
10. Once the cooking is complete, remove the Welsh Rarebit from Zone 1 and let it cool for a minute.
11. Cut each **Welsh Rarebit** slice into halves or desired shape. Serve the Welsh Rarebit hot, accompanied by a side salad or pickles.

Apple Chips

Prep: 10 Min | Cook: 45 Min | Serves: 4

Ingredient:

- 4 medium-sized apples
- Juice of 1 lemon
- Optional: cinnamon or sugar for sprinkling

▶ Instruction:

1. Wash and core the apples. Use a mandoline slicer or a sharp knife to slice the apples into thin, even rounds, about 3mm thick.
2. Place the apple slices in a bowl and squeeze the lemon juice over them. Toss gently to coat the slices evenly.
3. Arrange the apple slices in a single layer on both zones of the air fryer basket.
4. Select Zone 1 and choose the AIR FRY program. Set the temperature to 100°C and the time to 45 minutes. Select MATCH. Press the START/STOP button to begin cooking the apple chips.
5. After 30 minutes of cooking, open the air fryer and gently flip the apple slices to ensure even cooking.
6. Close the air fryer and continue cooking for the remaining 15 minutes, or until the apple chips are dry and crispy. Check for desired crispness and cook longer if needed.
7. Once the cooking is complete, remove the apple chips from Zone 1 and let them cool for a few minutes.
8. Sprinkle the apple chips with cinnamon or sugar, if desired.
9. Repeat the process with any remaining apple slices if needed.
10. Serve the **Apple Chips** as a healthy and delicious snack.
11. Instruction:

CHAPTER 05: SNACKS

Banana Bread Fritters

Prep: 15 Min | Cook: 10 Min | Serves: 4

Ingredient:

- 2 ripe bananas
- 100g self-raising flour
- 25g granulated sugar
- 1/2 teaspoon ground cinnamon
- 1/4 teaspoon ground nutmeg
- 1/4 teaspoon salt
- 1 large egg
- 60ml milk
- 1 teaspoon vanilla extract
- Vegetable oil, for greasing
- Optional toppings: icing sugar, maple syrup, whipped cream

▶ Instruction:

1. In a mixing bowl, mash the ripe bananas until smooth.
2. Add the self-raising flour, granulated sugar, ground cinnamon, ground nutmeg, and salt to the mashed bananas. Mix well to combine.
3. In a separate bowl, whisk together the egg, milk, and vanilla extract. Pour the egg mixture into the banana mixture and stir until a thick batter forms.
4. Lightly grease both zones of the air fryer basket with vegetable oil.
5. Drop spoonfuls of the batter into Zone 1 and Zone 2 of the air fryer basket, making sure to leave space between each fritter.
6. Select Zone 1 and choose the AIR FRY program. Set the temperature to 180°C and the time to 10 minutes. Select MATCH. Press the START/STOP.
7. After 5 minutes of cooking, open the air fryer and gently flip the fritters using tongs or a spatula to ensure even browning.
8. Close the air fryer and continue cooking for the remaining 5 minutes, or until the fritters are golden brown and cooked through.
9. Once the cooking is complete, remove the banana bread fritters from the air fryer and let them cool for a minute.
10. Serve the **Banana Bread Fritters** warm, dusted with icing sugar and drizzled with maple syrup. Optional: Serve with a dollop of whipped cream on top.

Calamari Rings

Prep: 20 Min | Cook: 10 Min | Serves: 4

Ingredient:

- 300g calamari rings
- 100g all-purpose flour
- 2 large eggs
- 50ml milk
- 1 teaspoon paprika
- 1/2 teaspoon garlic powder
- 1/4 teaspoon salt
- 1/4 teaspoon black pepper
- Vegetable oil, for greasing
- Lemon wedges, for serving
- Optional: tartar sauce or marinara sauce, for dipping

Instruction:

1. In a shallow dish, mix together the all-purpose flour, paprika, garlic powder, salt, and black pepper.
2. In another shallow dish, whisk together the eggs and milk until well combined.
3. Dip each calamari ring into the egg mixture, allowing any excess to drip off, then coat it in the flour mixture. Shake off any excess flour.
4. Lightly grease Zone 1 and Zone 2 of the air fryer basket with vegetable oil.
5. Place the coated calamari rings in a single layer on both zones of the air fryer basket, leaving space between each ring.
6. Select Zone 1 and choose the AIR FRY program. Set the temperature to 200°C and the time to 10 minutes. Select MATCH. Press the START/STOP.
7. After 5 minutes of cooking, open the air fryer and gently flip the calamari rings using tongs or a spatula to ensure even browning.
8. Close the air fryer and continue cooking for the remaining 5 minutes, or until the calamari rings are golden brown and crispy.
9. Once the cooking is complete, remove the calamari rings from the air fryer and let them cool for a minute.
10. Serve the **Calamari Rings** hot, accompanied by lemon wedges and your choice of tartar sauce or marinara sauce for dipping.

CHAPTER 05: SNACKS

Cheesy Bacon Fries

Prep: 10 Min | Cook: 20 Min | Serves: 4

Ingredient:

- 800g potatoes, cut into fries
- 200g grated cheddar cheese
- 150g bacon, cooked and crumbled
- 2 tablespoons vegetable oil
- 1 teaspoon paprika
- 1/2 teaspoon garlic powder
- 1/2 teaspoon onion powder
- Salt and pepper, to taste
- Fresh parsley or chives, chopped (for garnish)
- Optional: sour cream or ranch dressing (for dipping)

Instruction:

1. In a large bowl, combine the cut potatoes, vegetable oil, paprika, garlic powder, onion powder, salt, and pepper. Toss until the fries are evenly coated.
2. Arrange the seasoned fries in Zone 1 of the air fryer basket in a single layer, leaving space between each fry.
3. Select Zone 1 and choose the AIR FRY program. Set the temperature to 200°C and the time to 20 minutes. Press the START/STOP button to begin cooking the fries.
4. After 10 minutes of cooking, open the air fryer and gently shake the basket or use tongs to flip the fries for even cooking.
5. Close the air fryer and continue cooking for the remaining 10 minutes, or until the fries are golden brown and crispy.
6. Once the cooking is complete, transfer the fries from Zone 1 to a serving dish.
7. Sprinkle the grated cheddar cheese and crumbled bacon over the hot fries.
8. Place the dish with the cheese and bacon-topped fries in Zone 1 of the air fryer basket. Select Zone 1 and choose the AIR FRY program. Set the temperature to 200°C and the time to 3-5 minutes, or until the cheese is melted and bubbly.
9. Garnish the **Cheesy Bacon Fries** with fresh parsley or chives.
10. Serve the fries hot as a delicious snack or side dish. Optionally, serve with sour cream or ranch dressing for dipping.

Cheesy Nachos

Prep: 10 Min | Cook: 10 Min | Serves: 4

Ingredient:

- 200g tortilla chips
- 200g grated cheddar cheese
- 1 jalapeno pepper, sliced (optional)
- 1/2 red onion, finely diced
- 1 tomato, diced
- 2 tablespoons chopped fresh cilantro (coriander)
- 1/2 teaspoon ground cumin
- 1/2 teaspoon paprika
- 1/4 teaspoon garlic powder
- Salt and pepper, to taste
- Optional toppings: sour cream, guacamole, salsa

Instruction:

1. In a bowl, mix together the ground cumin, paprika, garlic powder, salt, and pepper.
2. Spread the tortilla chips evenly in Zone 1 of the air fryer basket.
3. Sprinkle half of the grated cheddar cheese over the tortilla chips.
4. Sprinkle half of the diced red onion, diced tomato, and sliced jalapeno (if using) over the cheese.
5. Repeat steps 2 to 4 to create another layer of chips, cheese, and toppings.
6. Select Zone 1 and choose the AIR FRY program. Set the temperature to 200°C and the time to 10 minutes. Press the START/STOP button to begin cooking the nachos.
7. After 5 minutes of cooking, open the air fryer and gently shake the basket or use tongs to stir the nachos, ensuring even melting of the cheese.
8. Close the air fryer and continue cooking for the remaining 5 minutes, or until the cheese is melted and bubbly.
9. Sprinkle the chopped fresh cilantro (coriander) over the hot cheesy nachos.
10. Serve the **Cheesy Nachos** immediately with optional toppings such as sour cream, guacamole, and salsa.

CHAPTER 05: SNACKS

Chicken Pakoras

Prep: 15 Min | Cook: 12 Min | Serves: 4

Ingredient:

- 500g boneless, skinless chicken breast, cut into bite-sized pieces
- 150g gram flour (chickpea flour)
- 1 teaspoon ground cumin
- 1 teaspoon ground coriander
- 1/2 teaspoon turmeric
- 1/2 teaspoon chili powder (adjust to taste)
- 1/2 teaspoon baking powder
- 1/2 teaspoon salt
- 1/4 teaspoon garam masala
- 1/4 teaspoon garlic powder
- 1/4 teaspoon onion powder
- 1 tablespoon lemon juice
- 150ml water
- Vegetable oil, for spraying

Instruction:

1. In a bowl, combine the gram flour, ground cumin, ground coriander, turmeric, chili powder, baking powder, salt, garam masala, garlic powder, and onion powder. Mix well.
2. Add the lemon juice and water to the dry ingredients. Stir until you have a smooth batter.
3. Dip the chicken pieces into the batter, making sure they are evenly coated.
4. Arrange the coated chicken pieces in Zone 1 of the air fryer basket in a single layer.
5. Select Zone 1 and choose the AIR FRY program. Set the temperature to 200°C and the time to 12 minutes. Press the START/STOP button to begin cooking the chicken pakoras.
6. After 6 minutes of cooking, open the air fryer and use tongs to flip the chicken pakoras for even browning.
7. Close the air fryer and continue cooking for the remaining 6 minutes, or until the chicken is cooked through and golden brown.
8. Serve the **Chicken Pakoras** hot as an appetizer or snack, with your favorite chutney or dipping sauce.

Chips and Curry Sauce

Prep: 15 Min | Cook: 30 Min | Serves: 4

Ingredient:

For the Chips:
- 800g potatoes, cut into chips
- 2 tablespoons vegetable oil
- Salt, to taste

For the Curry Sauce:
- 2 tablespoons vegetable oil
- 1 onion, finely chopped
- 2 cloves of garlic, minced
- 2 tablespoons curry powder
- 1 tablespoon plain flour
- 400ml chicken or vegetable stock
- 2 tablespoons tomato paste
- 1 tablespoon Worcestershire sauce
- Salt and pepper, to taste

Instruction:

1. In a bowl, toss the cut potatoes with vegetable oil and salt until evenly coated.
2. Arrange the seasoned chips in Zone 1 of the air fryer basket in a single layer.
3. Select Zone 1 and choose the AIR FRY program. Set the temperature to 200°C for 30 minutes. Press the START/STOP.
4. While the chips are cooking, prepare the curry sauce. Heat vegetable oil in a saucepan over medium heat. Add the chopped onion and minced garlic to the pan. Sauté until the onion becomes soft and translucent. Stir in the curry powder and plain flour, and cook for an additional 1-2 minutes to toast the spices.
5. Gradually pour in the chicken or vegetable stock, stirring constantly to avoid lumps. Add the tomato paste and Worcestershire sauce to the saucepan. Stir well to combine.
6. Simmer the curry sauce over low heat for about 10 minutes, or until it thickens to your desired consistency. Season with salt and pepper to taste.
7. Once the chips are ready, serve them hot with the homemade curry sauce.
8. Enjoy your **Chips and Curry Sauce** hot!

CHAPTER 05: SNACKS

Chocolate-Coated Nuts

Prep: 10 Min | Cook: 10 Min | Serves: 4

Ingredient:

- 200g mixed nuts (such as almonds, cashews, and peanuts)
- 200g dark or milk chocolate, chopped
- 1 tablespoon vegetable oil
- Optional toppings: sea salt, cocoa powder, shredded coconut

Instruction:

1. In a microwave-safe bowl, melt the chopped chocolate in the microwave in 30-second intervals, stirring in between, until smooth and fully melted. Alternatively, you can melt the chocolate using a double boiler on the stovetop.
2. Add the vegetable oil to the melted chocolate and stir well.
3. Place the mixed nuts in Zone 1 of the air fryer basket. Select Zone 1 and choose the AIR FRY program. Set the temperature to 160°C and the time to 10 minutes. Press the START/STOP.
4. After 5 minutes of toasting, open the air fryer and shake the basket. Close the air fryer and continue toasting the nuts for the remaining 5 minutes, or until they are golden brown and fragrant.
5. Once the nuts are toasted, transfer them from Zone 1 to a heatproof bowl. Pour the melted chocolate mixture over the toasted nuts and stir until all the nuts are evenly coated.
6. Spread the chocolate-coated nuts in a single layer in Zone 1. Select Zone 1 and choose the AIR FRY program. Set the temperature to 160°C for 5 minutes. Press the START/STOP.
7. Once the cooking is complete, remove the chocolate-coated nuts from Zone 1 and spread them on a parchment-lined tray or plate.
8. While the chocolate is still melted, sprinkle optional toppings such as sea salt, cocoa powder, or shredded coconut over the nuts for added flavor and texture. Allow the **chocolate-coated nuts** to cool and the chocolate to set completely before serving.

Crispy Tofu Bites

Prep: 20 Min | Cook: 20 Min | Serves: 4

Ingredient:

- 400g firm tofu, pressed and drained
- 2 tablespoons cornstarch
- 2 tablespoons nutritional yeast (optional)
- 1 teaspoon garlic powder
- 1 teaspoon paprika
- 1/2 teaspoon salt
- 1/4 teaspoon black pepper
- Vegetable oil, for spraying

➤ Instruction:

1. Cut the pressed tofu into bite-sized cubes, approximately 2cm in size.
2. In a bowl, combine the cornstarch, nutritional yeast (if using), garlic powder, paprika, salt, and black pepper. Mix well.
3. Toss the tofu cubes in the cornstarch mixture until they are evenly coated.
4. Arrange the coated tofu cubes in Zone 1 of the air fryer basket in a single layer, leaving space between each cube.
5. Select Zone 1 and choose the AIR FRY program. Set the temperature to 200°C and the time to 20 minutes. Press the START/STOP button to begin cooking the tofu bites.
6. After 10 minutes of cooking, open the air fryer and use tongs to flip the tofu bites for even browning.
7. Close the air fryer and continue cooking for the remaining 10 minutes, or until the tofu bites are crispy and golden brown.
8. Once the cooking is complete, remove the tofu bites from Zone 1.
9. Serve the **Crispy Tofu Bites** hot as a snack or as part of a meal. They can be enjoyed on their own or dipped in your favorite sauce.

CHAPTER 05: SNACKS

Fish Fingers

Prep: 15 Min | Cook: 12 Min | Serves: 4

Ingredient:

- 500g white fish fillets (such as cod or haddock), cut into finger-sized strips
- 100g all-purpose flour
- 2 eggs, beaten
- 150g breadcrumbs
- 1 teaspoon paprika
- 1/2 teaspoon garlic powder
- 1/2 teaspoon salt
- Vegetable oil, for spraying

➤ Instruction:

1. In three separate bowls, set up a breading station. Place the flour in the first bowl, beaten eggs in the second bowl, and breadcrumbs mixed with paprika, garlic powder, and salt in the third bowl.
2. Dip each fish finger into the flour, shaking off any excess. Then, dip it into the beaten eggs, allowing any excess to drip off. Finally, coat the fish finger in the breadcrumb mixture, pressing gently to adhere the breadcrumbs.
3. Place the breaded fish fingers in Zone 1 of the air fryer basket in a single layer, leaving space between each finger.
4. Select Zone 1 and choose the AIR FRY program. Set the temperature to 200°C and the time to 12 minutes. Press the START/STOP button to begin cooking the fish fingers.
5. After 6 minutes of cooking, open the air fryer and use tongs to flip the fish fingers for even browning.
6. Close the air fryer and continue cooking for the remaining 6 minutes, or until the fish fingers are crispy and golden brown.
7. Once the cooking is complete, remove the fish fingers from Zone 1.
8. Serve the **Fish Fingers** hot with your choice of dipping sauce, accompanied by chips or a side salad.

Mini Sausage Rolls

Prep: 20 Min | Cook: 15 Min | Serves: 24 rolls

Ingredient:

- 500g puff pastry, thawed if frozen
- 400g sausage meat
- 1 small onion, finely chopped
- 1 garlic clove, minced
- 1 teaspoon dried thyme
- 1 teaspoon dried parsley
- 1/2 teaspoon salt
- 1/4 teaspoon black pepper
- 1 egg, beaten (for egg wash)
- Sesame seeds, for sprinkling (optional)

Instruction:

1. In a bowl, combine the sausage meat, finely chopped onion, minced garlic, dried thyme, dried parsley, salt, and black pepper. Mix well until all the ingredients are thoroughly incorporated.
2. On a lightly floured surface, roll out the thawed puff pastry to a rectangle approximately 30cm x 40cm in size.
3. Cut the rolled-out puff pastry into 4 equal strips lengthwise. Divide the sausage meat mixture into 4 portions. Take one portion and shape it into a long log along the length of one of the pastry strips.
4. Brush one edge of each pastry strip with beaten egg. Roll the pastry over the sausage meat, enclosing it completely and sealing the edge with the egg-washed side. Cut each long roll into 6 equal-sized mini sausage rolls.
5. Place the mini sausage rolls in Zone 1 and Zone 2 of the air fryer basket, leaving space between each roll.
6. Select Zone 1 and choose the AIR FRY program. Set the temperature to 180°C and the time to 15 minutes. Select MATCH. Press the START/STOP.
7. After 7 minutes of cooking, open the air fryer and use tongs to carefully turn the mini sausage rolls for even browning. Close the air fryer and continue cooking for the remaining 8 minutes.
8. Serve the **Mini Sausage Rolls** warm as a delicious appetizer or snack.

CHAPTER 05: SNACKS

Mozzarella Sticks

Prep: 20 Min | Cook: 8 Min | Serves: 16 sticks

Ingredient:

- 250g mozzarella cheese, cut into sticks (approximately 1.5cm x 1.5cm x 7.5cm)
- 100g all-purpose flour
- 2 eggs, beaten
- 150g breadcrumbs
- 1 teaspoon dried oregano
- 1/2 teaspoon garlic powder
- 1/2 teaspoon salt
- Vegetable oil, for spraying

Instruction:

1. In three separate bowls, set up a breading station. Place the flour in the first bowl, beaten eggs in the second bowl, and breadcrumbs mixed with dried oregano, garlic powder, and salt in the third bowl.
2. Dip each mozzarella stick into the flour, shaking off any excess. Then, dip it into the beaten eggs, allowing any excess to drip off. Finally, coat the mozzarella stick in the breadcrumb mixture, pressing gently to adhere the breadcrumbs.
3. Place the breaded mozzarella sticks in Zone 1 and Zone 2 of the air fryer basket in a single layer, leaving space between each stick.
4. Select Zone 1 and choose the AIR FRY program. Set the temperature to 200°C and the time to 8 minutes. Select MATCH. Press the START/STOP button to begin cooking.
5. After 4 minutes of cooking, open the air fryer and use tongs to carefully turn the mozzarella sticks for even browning.
6. Close the air fryer and continue cooking for the remaining 4 minutes, or until the mozzarella sticks are golden brown and the cheese inside is melted.
7. Once the cooking is complete, remove the mozzarella sticks from Zone 1. Serve the **Mozzarella Sticks** hot with your favorite marinara sauce or dipping sauce.

Mushrooms on Toast

Prep: 10 Min | Cook: 10 Min | Serves: 2-3

Ingredient:

- 300g mushrooms, sliced
- 2 cloves garlic, minced
- 2 tbsp butter
- 2 tbsp olive oil
- 2 tbsp fresh parsley, chopped
- 1 tsp thyme leaves
- 1 tsp lemon juice
- Salt and pepper, to taste
- Slices of bread, toasted

Instruction:

1. In Zone 1, place the sliced mushrooms. Select Zone 1, choose the AIR FRY program, and set the temperature to 180°C. Set the time to 8 minutes. Press the START/STOP button to begin air frying the mushrooms. This will help cook and tenderize them.
2. While the mushrooms are air frying, in a separate pan, heat the butter and olive oil over medium heat.
3. Add minced garlic to the pan and saute until fragrant.
4. In Zone 1, pour the sautéed garlic, butter, and olive oil mixture from the pan over the mushrooms in Zone 1.
5. Sprinkle the fresh parsley, thyme leaves, lemon juice, salt, and pepper over the mushrooms.
6. Select Zone 1, choose the ROAST program, and set the temperature to 180°C. Set the time to 2 minutes.
7. Press the START/STOP button to begin roasting the Mushrooms on Toast.
8. After 2 minutes of roasting, carefully remove the Mushrooms on Toast from the air fryer.
9. Serve the **mushrooms** on slices of toasted bread.
10. Optionally, garnish with additional fresh parsley before serving.

CHAPTER 05: SNACKS

Onion Bhajis

Prep: 15 Min | Cook: 10 Min | Serves: 4

Ingredient:

- 2 large onions, thinly sliced
- 100g gram flour (chickpea flour)
- 1 teaspoon ground cumin
- 1 teaspoon ground coriander
- 1/2 teaspoon turmeric
- 1/2 teaspoon chili powder (optional, adjust to taste)
- 1/2 teaspoon baking powder
- 1/2 teaspoon salt
- 1/4 teaspoon black pepper
- 120ml water
- Vegetable oil, for greasing

Instruction:

1. In a large bowl, combine the gram flour, ground cumin, ground coriander, turmeric, chili powder (if using), baking powder, salt, and black pepper.
2. Gradually add water to the dry ingredients, stirring well to form a smooth batter. The batter should be thick enough to coat the onion slices.
3. Add the thinly sliced onions to the batter and mix until all the onion slices are well coated.
4. In Zone 1 of the air fryer, lightly grease the surface with vegetable oil. Select Zone 1, choose the AIR FRY program, and set the temperature to 200°C. Set the time to 2 minutes. Press the START/STOP button to begin preheating.
5. Once the air fryer is preheated, carefully spoon small portions of the onion mixture into both zone to form small bhajis. Make sure to leave some space between each bhaji.
6. Select Zone 1, choose the AIR FRY program, and set the temperature to 200°C. Set the time to 10 minutes. Select MATCH. Press the START/STOP.
7. Close the air fryer and cook the bhajis for 10 minutes, or until they are golden brown and crispy.
8. While the first batch of bhajis is cooking, continue shaping the remaining bhajis with the remaining batter. Once the batch is cooked, transfer the **bhajis** to a plate lined with kitchen paper to drain any excess oil.

Potato Skins

Prep: 15 Min | Cook: 40 Min | Serves: 4

Ingredient:

- 4 medium-sized potatoes (about 700g)
- 100g grated cheddar cheese
- 100g bacon, cooked and crumbled
- 2 spring onions, finely chopped
- 50g sour cream
- Salt and pepper to taste

➤ Instruction:

1. Thoroughly wash and dry the potatoes. Pierce them with a fork.
2. Place the potatoes in Zone 1. Select Zone 1, choose the AIR FRY program, and set the temperature to 200°C. Set the time to 40 minutes. Press the START/STOP .
3. While the potatoes are cooking, prepare the toppings. Cook the bacon until crispy, then crumble it into small pieces. Finely chop the spring onions and set aside. Prepare any additional toppings you desire.
4. After 20 minutes, pause air fryer, flip potatoes for even cooking.
5. Once the potatoes are cooked, remove them from the air fryer and let them cool slightly. Cut each potato in half lengthwise. Use a spoon to scoop out most of the flesh, leaving a thin layer attached to the skin. Save the scooped-out flesh for another use.
6. Place the hollowed-out potato skins in Zone 1. Choose the AIR FRY program, and set the temperature to 200°C. Set the time to 5 minutes to crisp up the skins.
7. While the skins are crisping, season them with salt and pepper. Fill each skin with a sprinkle of grated cheddar cheese and bacon crumbles. Return the filled potato skins back to Zone 1 of the air fryer and cook for an additional 3-5 minutes, or until the cheese is melted and bubbly.
8. Serve the **Potato Skins** hot, topped with chopped spring onions and a dollop of sour cream.

CHAPTER 05: SNACKS

Prawn Cocktail Skewers

Prep: 10 Min | Cook: 6 Min | Serves: 4

Ingredient:

- 300g cooked and peeled prawns
- 4 tablespoons mayonnaise
- 2 tablespoons tomato ketchup
- 1 tablespoon lemon juice
- 1 teaspoon Worcestershire sauce
- 1/2 teaspoon paprika
- Salt and pepper, to taste
- 1 small iceberg lettuce, shredded
- 1 avocado, diced
- 1 small cucumber, sliced
- 8 cherry tomatoes
- 4 wooden skewers

➤ Instruction:

1. In a bowl, combine the mayonnaise, tomato ketchup, lemon juice, Worcestershire sauce, paprika, salt, and pepper. Mix well to make the Marie Rose sauce.
2. Thread the prawns onto the wooden skewers, alternating with cherry tomatoes.
3. Evenly dividing prawn skewers between the two zone, leaving space between each skewer.
4. Select Zone 1, set the time to 5-6 minutes at 200°C on the AIR FRY program. Select MATCH. Press the START/STOP.
5. After 2-3 minutes of cooking, check the prawn skewers for desired crispness. If needed, continue cooking for another minute or two.
6. While the prawn skewers cook, prepare the salad. In a bowl, combine the shredded iceberg lettuce, diced avocado, and sliced cucumber.
7. Once the prawn skewers are cooked, carefully remove them from the air fryer basket.
8. Serve the **prawn skewers** on top of the salad, and drizzle the Marie Rose sauce over the top.

Samosas

Prep: 30 Min | Cook: 15 Min | Serves: 12 samosas

Ingredient:

For the dough:
- 250g plain flour
- 1/2 tsp salt
- 2 tbsp vegetable oil
- 125ml warm water

For the filling:
- 300g potatoes, boiled and mashed
- 100g peas, boiled and mashed
- 1 small onion, finely chopped
- 2 cloves garlic, minced
- 1 tsp grated ginger
- 1 tsp ground cumin
- 1 tsp ground coriander
- 1/2 tsp garam masala
- 1/2 tsp turmeric powder
- Salt, to taste
- Vegetable oil, for frying

▶ Instruction:

1. In a mixing bowl, combine the plain flour and salt for the dough. Mix well. Add the vegetable oil to the flour mixture and mix until it resembles breadcrumbs. Gradually add the warm water and knead until a smooth dough is formed. Cover the dough and let it rest for 15 minutes.
2. In a separate bowl, combine the mashed potatoes, mashed peas, chopped onion, minced garlic, grated ginger, ground cumin, ground coriander, garam masala, turmeric powder, and salt for the filling. Mix well.
3. Divide the dough into 12 equal-sized portions and roll each portion into a ball. On a lightly floured surface, roll out each dough ball into a thin circle of about 15cm in diameter. Cut each rolled out dough circle in half to create semi-circles.
4. Take one semi-circle and fold it into a cone shape, overlapping the edges. Seal the edges with a little water. Fill the cone-shaped dough with about 2 tablespoons of the potato and pea filling. Press it down gently. Apply water to the open edge of the cone and seal it tightly.
5. Evenly dividing samosas between the two zone, leaving space between them. Select Zone 1, choose the AIR FRY program, and set the temperature to 200°C. Set the time to 15 minutes. Select MATCH. Press the START/STOP.
6. Serve the **samosas** hot with your choice of chutney or dipping sauce.

CHAPTER 05: SNACKS

Sweet Potato Fries

Prep: 15 Min | Cook: 20 Min | Serves: 4

Ingredient:

- 500g sweet potatoes
- 2 tablespoons cornstarch
- 2 tablespoons olive oil
- 1/2 teaspoon paprika
- 1/2 teaspoon garlic powder
- 1/2 teaspoon salt
- 1/4 teaspoon black pepper
- Cooking spray or additional oil, for greasing

▶ Instruction:

1. Peel the sweet potatoes and cut them into long, thin strips, about 1 cm thick.
2. Place the sweet potato strips in a large bowl of cold water and let them soak for 10 minutes to remove excess starch. Drain and pat dry using a clean kitchen towel or paper towels.
3. In a separate bowl, combine the cornstarch, olive oil, paprika, garlic powder, salt, and black pepper. Mix well to form a paste.
4. Add the sweet potato strips to the bowl with the cornstarch mixture. Toss until the sweet potato strips are evenly coated.
5. Lightly grease the air fryer basket with cooking spray or a small amount of oil in both zone.
6. Evenly dividing coated sweet potato strips between the two zone, making sure they are in a single layer and not overcrowded.
7. Select Zone 1, choose the AIR FRY program, and set the temperature to 200°C. Set the time to 20 minutes. Select MATCH. Press the START/STOP button to begin cooking.
8. After 10 minutes, open the air fryer and shake the basket to flip the sweet potato fries for even cooking.
9. Once cooked, carefully remove the sweet potato fries from the air fryer and let them cool slightly.
10. Serve the **Sweet Potato Fries** as a tasty side dish or snack.

Baked Camembert

Prep: 5 Min | Cook: 15 Min | Serves: 4

Ingredient:

- 1 whole Camembert cheese (about 250g)
- 2 cloves garlic, thinly sliced
- 2 sprigs fresh thyme
- 1 tablespoon olive oil
- Freshly ground black pepper, to taste
- Bread or crackers, for serving

➤ Instruction:

1. Remove any plastic packaging from the Camembert cheese. Place the cheese on a piece of parchment paper or aluminum foil.
2. Using a sharp knife, make shallow cuts or slits on the top of the cheese. Insert the thinly sliced garlic and fresh thyme sprigs into the slits.
3. Drizzle the olive oil over the top of the cheese. Season with freshly ground black pepper to taste.
4. In Zone 1 of the air fryer, place the Camembert cheese with its parchment paper or aluminum foil. Select Zone 1, choose the BAKE program, and set the temperature to 180°C. Set the time to 12-15 minutes.
5. Press the START/STOP button to begin cooking.
6. Once the air fryer has preheated, close the air fryer and cook the Camembert cheese for 12-15 minutes, or until the cheese is soft and gooey in the center.
7. Carefully remove the baked Camembert from the air fryer and let it cool for a few minutes.
8. Serve the baked **Camembert** with bread or crackers for dipping and spreading. You can also garnish it with additional fresh thyme if desired.

CHAPTER 06: SUNDAY AND HOLIDAY

Baked Stuffed Apples

Prep: 10 Min | Cook: 20 Min | Serves: 4

Ingredient:

- 4 apples
- 50g butter, melted
- 50g rolled oats
- 50g chopped almonds
- 50g dried cranberries
- 2 tablespoons honey
- 1 teaspoon ground cinnamon
- 1/4 teaspoon ground nutmeg
- Vanilla ice cream, for serving (optional)

➤ Instruction:

1. Cut off the top of each apple and scoop out the core and seeds with a spoon.
2. In a bowl, mix together melted butter, rolled oats, chopped almonds, dried cranberries, honey, ground cinnamon, and ground nutmeg.
3. Stuff the mixture into each apple, filling them to the top.
4. Place the apples in Zone 1 of the air fryer.
5. Select Zone 1, choose the ROAST program, and set the temperature to 180°C. Set the time to 20 minutes.
6. Press the START/STOP button to begin cooking.
7. Once the apples are cooked through and the topping is golden brown, remove from the air fryer and let cool for a few minutes.
8. Serve your delicious **Baked Stuffed Apples** with a scoop of vanilla ice cream, if desired. Enjoy!

Braised Red Cabbage

Prep: 10 Min | Cook: 40 Min | Serves: 4

Ingredient:

- 1 small red cabbage, finely shredded (about 600g)
- 2 tablespoons butter
- 1 onion, thinly sliced
- 2 apples, peeled, cored, and chopped
- 2 tablespoons brown sugar
- 2 tablespoons red wine vinegar
- 250 ml vegetable or beef broth
- 1 bay leaf
- Salt and pepper, to taste

Instruction:

1. In Zone 1 of the air fryer, melt the butter. Select Zone 1, choose the AIR FRY program, and set the temperature to 180°C. Set the time to 5 minutes.
2. Press the START/STOP button to begin preheating.
3. Add the sliced onion to Zone 1 and cook until softened and lightly browned.
4. Stir in the chopped apples and cook for an additional 2 minutes.
5. In Zone 2 of the air fryer, place the finely shredded red cabbage. Select Zone 2, choose the AIR FRY program, and set the temperature to 180°C. Set the time to 10 minutes.
6. Press the START/STOP button to begin cooking.
7. After 10 minutes, open the air fryer and give the cabbage a stir. Add the brown sugar, red wine vinegar, vegetable or beef broth, bay leaf, salt, and pepper. Stir to combine.
8. Close the air fryer and continue cooking the cabbage for an additional 25 minutes, or until it is tender and has absorbed most of the liquid.
9. Carefully remove the braised red cabbage from the air fryer and discard the bay leaf.
10. Serve the **braised red cabbage** as a side dish with your desired main course.

CHAPTER 06: SUNDAY AND HOLIDAY

Cabbage Rolls

Prep: 30 Min | Cook: 30 Min | Serves: 4

Ingredient:

- 1 head of cabbage
- 500g ground beef
- 1 onion, finely chopped
- 2 cloves garlic, minced
- 1 carrot, grated
- 100g cooked rice
- 1 tablespoon tomato paste
- 1 teaspoon dried thyme
- 1 teaspoon dried oregano
- Salt and pepper, to taste
- 400g can of diced tomatoes
- 250 ml beef broth
- Fresh parsley, chopped (for garnish)

Instruction:

1. Fill a large pot with water and bring it to a boil. Add the whole head of cabbage and cook for 8-10 minutes, or until the outer leaves are tender and pliable.
2. Remove the cabbage from the pot and carefully peel off the individual leaves. Trim the tough center rib from each leaf.
3. In Zone 1 of the air fryer, cook the ground beef, onion, and garlic until the beef is browned and the onion is softened. Select Zone 1, choose the AIR FRY program, and set the temperature to 180°C. Set the time to 10 minutes.
4. Press the START/STOP button to begin cooking.
5. In a bowl, combine the cooked ground beef mixture, grated carrot, cooked rice, tomato paste, dried thyme, dried oregano, salt, and pepper. Mix well to combine.
6. Place a spoonful of the beef mixture onto the center of each cabbage leaf. Roll up the leaf, tucking in the sides as you go, to form a cabbage roll. Repeat with the remaining leaves and filling.
7. In Zone 1 of the air fryer, place the cabbage rolls seam-side down. Select Zone 1, choose the AIR FRY program, and set the temperature to 180°C. Set the time to 20 minutes.
8. Press the START/STOP button to begin cooking.
9. After 20 minutes, open the air fryer and pour the diced tomatoes and beef broth over the cabbage rolls. Carefully remove the **cabbage rolls** from the air fryer and garnish with fresh chopped parsley.

Cauliflower Cheese

Prep: 15 Min | Cook: 20 Min | Serves: 4

Ingredient:

- 1 medium-sized cauliflower (about 800g), cut into florets
- 50g unsalted butter
- 50g plain flour
- 500ml whole milk
- 200g grated cheddar cheese
- Salt and pepper to taste
- Optional: 2 tablespoons breadcrumbs

▶ Instruction:

1. Bring a large saucepan of salted water to a boil. Add the cauliflower florets and cook for 5-7 minutes, or until they are just tender. Drain the cauliflower and set aside.
2. In a separate saucepan, melt the butter over medium heat. Add the flour and cook, stirring constantly, for 2-3 minutes to make a roux.
3. Gradually whisk in the milk, ensuring there are no lumps. Cook the mixture, stirring constantly, until it thickens to a smooth sauce.
4. Reduce the heat to low and stir in 150g of grated cheddar cheese until melted. Season the sauce with salt and pepper to taste.
5. Place the cooked cauliflower florets in Zone 1. Select Zone 1, choose the AIR FRY program, set the temperature to 180°C, Set time to 5 minutes to warm up the cauliflower. Press the START/STOP button to begin cooking.
6. After 5 minutes, pour the cheese sauce over the cauliflower, ensuring all the florets are coated.
7. Sprinkle the remaining of grated cheddar cheese (and breadcrumbs, if using) evenly over the cauliflower.
8. Place the cauliflower cheese in Zone 1. Select Zone 1, choose the AIR FRY program, and set the temperature to 180°C. Set the time to 15 minutes to melt the cheese and brown the top.
9. Press the START/STOP button to begin cooking. Once cooked, remove the **cauliflower cheese** from the air fryer and let it cool for a few minutes before serving.

CHAPTER 06: SUNDAY AND HOLIDAY

Corned Beef Hash

Prep: 15 Min | Cook: 25 Min | Serves: 4

Ingredient:

- 500g potatoes, peeled and diced
- 1 onion, finely chopped
- 200g cooked corned beef, diced
- 2 tablespoons vegetable oil
- 1 teaspoon Worcestershire sauce
- Salt and pepper, to taste
- Fresh parsley, chopped (for garnish)
- Fried eggs (optional, for serving)

▶ Instruction:

1. In Zone 1 of the air fryer, cook the diced potatoes until they are golden brown and crispy. Select Zone 1, choose the AIR FRY program, and set the temperature to 180°C. Set the time to 20 minutes.
2. Press the START/STOP button to begin cooking.
3. In Zone 2 of the air fryer, cook the chopped onion until it is softened and lightly browned. Select Zone 2, choose the AIR FRY program, and set the temperature to 180°C. Set the time to 5 minutes. Press the START/STOP button to begin cooking.
4. In a large bowl, combine the cooked potatoes, cooked onions, diced corned beef, vegetable oil, Worcestershire sauce, salt, and pepper. Mix well to combine.
5. Divide the mixture into four equal portions and shape them into patties.
6. In Zone 1, place the corned beef hash patties. Select Zone 1, choose the AIR FRY program, and set the temperature to 180°C. Set the time to 5 minutes. Press the START/STOP.
7. After 5 minutes, open the air fryer and carefully flip the corned beef hash patties. Close the air fryer and continue cooking for an additional 5 minutes, or until the patties are heated through and crispy on the outside.
8. Carefully remove the **corned beef hash** patties from the air fryer and garnish with fresh chopped parsley.
9. Serve the corned beef hash patties with fried eggs, if desired.

Cornish Pasty

Prep: 30 Min | Cook: 20 Min | Serves: 4 patties

Ingredient:

- 300g shortcrust pastry
- 200g beef steak, diced
- 1 medium potato, peeled and diced
- 1 small onion, finely chopped
- 100g swede (rutabaga), peeled and diced
- Salt and pepper, to taste
- 1 egg, beaten (for egg wash)

▶ Instruction:

1. Roll out the shortcrust pastry on a lightly floured surface to about 3mm thickness. Cut out four circles, approximately 20cm in diameter.
2. In a bowl, combine the diced beef steak, potato, onion, and swede. Season with salt and pepper to taste.
3. Divide the beef and vegetable mixture into four equal portions. Place one portion on half of each pastry circle, leaving a border around the edges.
4. Brush the edges of each pastry circle with beaten egg. Fold the other half of the pastry over the filling, pressing the edges together. Crimp the edges to create a traditional pasty shape.
5. Place the pasties in Zone 1 of the air fryer basket, leaving space between each pasty.
6. Select Zone 1 and choose the AIR FRY program. Set the temperature to 200°C and the time to 20 minutes. Press the START/STOP button to begin cooking the Cornish pasties.
7. After 10 minutes of cooking, open the air fryer and use tongs to carefully turn the pasties for even browning. Close the air fryer and continue cooking for the remaining 10 minutes, or until the pasties are golden brown and the filling is cooked through.
8. Serve the **Cornish Pasty** warm as a hearty main course, accompanied by your favorite condiments or side dishes.

CHAPTER 06: SUNDAY AND HOLIDAY

Glazed Carrots

Prep: 10 Min | Cook: 15 Min | Serves: 4

Ingredient:

- 500g carrots, peeled and cut into 1cm thick slices
- 30g unsalted butter
- 2 tablespoons brown sugar
- 1 tablespoon honey
- 1/2 teaspoon salt
- 1/4 teaspoon black pepper
- Fresh parsley, chopped (for garnish)

▶ Instruction:

1. In Zone 1 of the air fryer basket, place the carrot slices in a single layer.
2. Select Zone 1 and choose the AIR FRY program. Set the temperature to 180°C and the time to 15 minutes. Press the START/STOP button to begin cooking the carrots.
3. After 7 minutes of cooking, open the air fryer and use tongs to carefully toss the carrot slices for even cooking.
4. Close the air fryer and continue cooking for the remaining 8 minutes, or until the carrots are tender.
5. While the carrots are cooking, melt the unsalted butter in a small saucepan over low heat. Stir in the brown sugar, honey, salt, and black pepper until well combined. Keep the glaze warm.
6. Once the cooking is complete, remove the carrots from Zone 1.
7. Drizzle the warm glaze over the cooked carrots and toss gently to coat them evenly.
8. Transfer the glazed carrots to a serving dish, garnish with chopped fresh parsley, and serve immediately.
9. Enjoy the **Glazed Carrots** as a flavorful and vibrant side dish with your favorite Sunday roast or holiday meal.

Grilled Asparagus

Prep: 10 Min | Cook: 6 Min | Serves: 4

Ingredient:

- 500g asparagus spears
- 2 tbsp olive oil
- 2 cloves garlic, minced
- Salt and pepper, to taste
- Lemon wedges, for serving

➤ Instruction:

1. Trim the tough ends of the asparagus spears, about 2-3cm from the bottom.
2. In a mixing bowl, combine the olive oil, minced garlic, salt, and pepper.
3. Toss the asparagus spears in the olive oil mixture until well coated.
4. Place the asparagus spears in Zone 1 of the Ninja Dual Zone Air Fryer, leaving space between them for even cooking.
5. Select Zone 1, choose the AIR FRY program, and set the temperature to 200°C. Set the time to 6 minutes.
6. Press the START/STOP button to begin air frying the asparagus.
7. After 3 minutes of air frying, carefully open the air fryer and shake the asparagus spears to ensure even cooking. Close the air fryer and continue cooking.
8. Once the cooking time is complete, carefully remove the grilled asparagus from the air fryer.
9. Serve the **grilled asparagus** hot with lemon wedges on the side.

CHAPTER 06: SUNDAY AND HOLIDAY

Honey Glazed Ham

Prep: 10 Min | Cook: 25 Min | Serves: 8

Ingredient:

- 1.5kg boneless cooked ham
- 100g brown sugar
- 3 tbsp honey
- 2 tbsp Dijon mustard
- 1 tbsp apple cider vinegar
- 1 tsp ground cinnamon
- 1/2 tsp ground cloves
- Whole cloves, for garnish

➤ Instruction:

1. In a small bowl, combine the brown sugar, honey, Dijon mustard, apple cider vinegar, ground cinnamon, and ground cloves. Mix well to form a glaze.
2. Place the boneless cooked ham in Zone 1 of the Ninja Dual Zone Air Fryer.
3. Select Zone 1, choose the AIR FRY program, and set the temperature to 180°C. Set the time to 15 minutes.
4. Press the START/STOP button to begin air frying the ham.
5. After 15 minutes, carefully open the air fryer and brush the glaze mixture over the ham, making sure to cover all sides.
6. Insert whole cloves into the surface of the ham for added flavor and presentation.
7. Close the air fryer and continue cooking for an additional 10 minutes.
8. Once the cooking time is complete, carefully remove the honey glazed ham from the air fryer.
9. Let the ham rest for a few minutes before slicing.
10. Serve the **honey glazed ham** warm as a delicious main dish or use it to make sandwiches or salads.

Lemon Tart

Prep: 30 Min | Cook: 20 Min | Serves: 6-8

Ingredient:

For the crust:
- 200g digestive biscuits
- 100g unsalted butter, melted

For the filling:
- 4 large eggs
- 150g granulated sugar
- Zest of 2 lemons
- Juice of 3 lemons
- 150ml double cream

▶ Instruction:

1. In a food processor, crush the digestive biscuits until they turn into fine crumbs. Add the melted butter and pulse until well combined.
2. Press the biscuit mixture firmly into a 20cm tart pan, ensuring an even layer on the bottom and up the sides. Place the tart pan in Zone 1 of the air fryer basket.
3. Select Zone 1 and choose the AIR FRY program. Set the temperature to 180°C for 8 minutes. Press the START/STOP.
4. After 8 minutes of cooking, open the air fryer and check if the crust is golden brown. If needed, cook for an additional 2 minutes until the desired color is achieved.
5. In a mixing bowl, whisk together the eggs, granulated sugar, lemon zest, lemon juice, and double cream until well combined.
6. Pour the lemon filling into the cooled tart crust. Place the tart pan back into Zone 1 of the air fryer basket.
7. Select Zone 1 and choose the AIR FRY program. Set the temperature to 180°C for 12 minutes. Press the START/STOP.
8. After 6 minutes of cooking, open the air fryer and use a toothpick or skewer to gently swirl the filling for even cooking. Close the air fryer and continue cooking for the remaining 6 minutes.
9. Transfer the tart to a wire rack to cool completely, then refrigerate for at least 2 hours before serving. Serve the **Lemon Tart** chilled, garnished with fresh lemon zest or a dusting of icing sugar.

CHAPTER 06: SUNDAY AND HOLIDAY

Mashed Potatoes

Prep: 10 Min | Cook: 20 Min | Serves: 4

Ingredient:

- 800g potatoes, peeled and cut into chunks
- 50g unsalted butter
- 100ml milk
- Salt, to taste
- Pepper, to taste
- Chopped fresh chives or parsley (for garnish)

▶ Instruction:

1. In Zone 1 of the air fryer basket, place the potato chunks in a single layer.
2. Select Zone 1 and choose the AIR FRY program. Set the temperature to 180°C and the time to 20 minutes. Press the START/STOP button to begin cooking the potatoes.
3. After 10 minutes of cooking, open the air fryer and use tongs to carefully toss the potato chunks for even browning.
4. Close the air fryer and continue cooking for the remaining 10 minutes, or until the potatoes are fork-tender and golden brown on the outside.
5. Once the cooking is complete, remove the potatoes from Zone 1 and transfer them to a large mixing bowl.
6. Add the unsalted butter, milk, salt, and pepper to the bowl of cooked potatoes.
7. Mash the potatoes using a potato masher or a fork until smooth and creamy. Adjust the seasoning if needed.
8. Transfer the mashed potatoes to a serving dish, garnish with chopped fresh chives or parsley, and serve immediately.
9. Enjoy the **Mashed Potatoes** as a comforting and classic side dish to complement your British meals.

Pigs in Blankets

Prep: 10 Min | Cook: 15 Min | Serves: 12

Ingredient:

- 12 chipolata sausages
- 6 rashers of streaky bacon, cut in half
- 1 tbsp vegetable oil
- 1 tbsp honey or maple syrup (optional, for glazing)

Instruction:

1. Wrap each chipolata sausage with half a rasher of streaky bacon, making sure to secure the bacon with toothpicks if necessary.
2. Evenly dividing wrapped sausages between the two zone, leaving space between them for even cooking.
3. Select Zone 1, choose the AIR FRY program, and set the temperature to 200°C. Set the time to 15 minutes. Select MATCH to duplicate settings across both zones.
4. Press the START/STOP button to begin air frying the pigs in blankets.
5. After 10 minutes of air frying, remove the toothpicks if used and brush the sausages with vegetable oil for a crispy finish.
6. If desired, drizzle honey or maple syrup over the pigs in blankets for a sweet glaze.
7. Close the air fryer and continue cooking for the remaining 5 minutes.
8. Once the cooking time is complete, carefully remove the pigs in blankets from the air fryer.
9. Serve the **pigs in blankets** hot as a delightful appetizer or side dish.

CHAPTER 06: SUNDAY AND HOLIDAY

Ratatouille

Prep: 15 Min | Cook: 25 Min | Serves: 4

Ingredient:

- 1 medium eggplant, cut into 2cm cubes
- 1 medium zucchini, cut into 2cm cubes
- 1 red bell pepper, cut into 2cm pieces
- 1 yellow bell pepper, cut into 2cm pieces
- 1 red onion, sliced
- 3 cloves garlic, minced
- 400g canned diced tomatoes
- 2 tbsp olive oil
- 1 tsp dried thyme
- 1 tsp dried basil
- Salt and pepper, to taste

Instruction:

1. In a large bowl, combine the eggplant, zucchini, red bell pepper, yellow bell pepper, red onion, minced garlic, olive oil, dried thyme, dried basil, salt, and pepper. Toss well to coat the vegetables.
2. Evenly dividing vegetable mixture between the two zone, leaving space between them for even cooking.
3. Select Zone 1, choose the AIR FRY program, and set the temperature to 180°C. Set the time to 25 minutes. Select MATCH to duplicate settings across both zones.
4. Press the START/STOP button to begin air frying the ratatouille.
5. After 10 minutes of air frying, carefully open the air fryer and give the vegetables a stir to ensure even cooking. Close the air fryer and continue cooking.
6. Once the cooking time is complete, carefully remove the ratatouille from the air fryer.
7. Serve the **ratatouille** hot as a delicious vegetarian main dish or as a side dish to accompany your favorite protein.

Salmon En Croute

Prep: 20 Min | Cook: 30 Min | Serves: 4

Ingredient:

- 500g puff pastry, thawed if frozen
- 600g salmon fillet, skinless
- 200g fresh spinach leaves
- 100g cream cheese
- 1 tablespoon Dijon mustard
- Salt and pepper, to taste
- 1 egg, beaten (for egg wash)

➤ Instruction:

1. Roll out the puff pastry on a lightly floured surface to approximately 30cm x 40cm in size.
2. In Zone 1 of the air fryer basket, place the salmon fillet and season it with salt and pepper.
3. Select Zone 1 and choose the AIR FRY program. Set the temperature to 200°C for 8 minutes. Press the START/STOP.
4. In a separate pan, wilt the fresh spinach leaves over medium heat until they have reduced in size. Set aside.
5. In a small bowl, mix the cream cheese and Dijon mustard until well combined. On the rolled-out puff pastry, spread a layer of the cream cheese and Dijon mustard mixture. Place the wilted spinach on top of the cream cheese mixture.
6. Once the cooked salmon has cooled slightly, place it on top of the spinach layer. Carefully fold the puff pastry over the salmon, sealing the edges to create a parcel.
7. Place the salmon en croute in Zone 2 of the air fryer basket.
8. Select Zone 2 and choose the AIR FRY program. Set the temperature to 200°C for 20 minutes. Press the START/STOP.
9. After 10 minutes of cooking, brush the pastry with the beaten egg wash. Continue cooking for the remaining 10 minutes.
10. Remove the salmon en croute from the air fryer and let it rest for a few minutes. Slice into portions and serve the **Salmon En Croute** warm with a side salad or your favorite vegetables.

CHAPTER 06: SUNDAY AND HOLIDAY

Scalloped Potatoes

Prep: 15 Min | Cook: 30 Min | Serves: 4

Ingredient:

- 800g potatoes, peeled and thinly sliced
- 300ml double cream
- 150g cheddar cheese, grated
- 1 small onion, finely chopped
- 2 garlic cloves, minced
- Salt, to taste
- Pepper, to taste
- Fresh thyme leaves (optional, for garnish)

➤ Instruction:

1. In a mixing bowl, combine the sliced potatoes, chopped onion, minced garlic, half of the grated cheddar cheese, double cream, salt, and pepper. Mix well to ensure the potatoes are coated.
2. Transfer the potato mixture to Zone 1 of the air fryer basket, spreading it out evenly.
3. Select Zone 1 and choose the AIR FRY program. Set the temperature to 180°C and the time to 30 minutes. Press the START/STOP button to begin cooking the potatoes.
4. After 20 minutes of cooking, open the air fryer and sprinkle the remaining grated cheddar cheese on top of the partially cooked potatoes.
5. Close the air fryer and continue cooking for the remaining 10 minutes, or until the potatoes are tender and the cheese is melted and golden brown.
6. Once the cooking is complete, remove the **Scalloped Potatoes** from Zone 1 and let them cool for a few minutes.
7. Garnish with fresh thyme leaves (if desired) and serve the Scalloped Potatoes warm as a comforting side dish to complement your British meals.

Stuffing Balls

Prep: 15 Min | Cook: 15 Min | Serves: 8

Ingredient:

- 250g breadcrumbs
- 1 medium onion, finely chopped
- 2 cloves garlic, minced
- 2 celery stalks, finely chopped
- 2 tbsp butter
- 1 tsp dried sage
- 1 tsp dried thyme
- 1 tsp dried parsley
- 1/2 tsp salt
- 1/4 tsp black pepper
- 1 large egg, beaten
- 120ml vegetable or chicken stock

Instruction:

1. In a large skillet, melt the butter over medium heat. Add the chopped onion, minced garlic, and celery, and sauté until softened, about 5 minutes.
2. In a large mixing bowl, combine the breadcrumbs, dried sage, dried thyme, dried parsley, salt, and black pepper.
3. Add the sautéed onion, garlic, and celery mixture to the bowl with the breadcrumbs. Mix well to combine.
4. Pour in the beaten egg and vegetable or chicken stock. Stir until the mixture is well combined and holds together when pressed.
5. Shape the stuffing mixture into golf ball-sized balls. Evenly dividing them between the two zone, ensuring they are in a single layer and not too crowded.
6. Select Zone 1, choose the AIR FRY program, and set the temperature to 180°C. Set the time to 15 minutes. Select MATCH. Press the START/STOP button to begin air frying the stuffing balls.
7. After 10 minutes of air frying, carefully open the air fryer and turn the stuffing balls to ensure even browning. Close the air fryer and continue cooking.
8. Once the cooking time is complete, carefully remove the stuffing balls from the air fryer.
9. Serve the **stuffing balls** hot as a delicious side dish to accompany your roast dinner or holiday meal.:

CHAPTER 06: SUNDAY AND HOLIDAY

Yam Fries

Prep: 10 Min | Cook: 20 Min | Serves: 4

Ingredient:

- 500g yams (or sweet potatoes), peeled and cut into fries
- 2 tablespoons olive oil
- 1 teaspoon paprika
- 1/2 teaspoon garlic powder
- 1/2 teaspoon onion powder
- 1/2 teaspoon salt
- 1/4 teaspoon black pepper
- Fresh parsley, chopped (for garnish)

Instruction:

1. In a large bowl, combine the yam fries, olive oil, paprika, garlic powder, onion powder, salt, and black pepper. Toss until the fries are evenly coated with the seasonings.
2. In Zone 1 of the air fryer, spread out the yam fries in a single layer. Select Zone 1, choose the AIR FRY program, and set the temperature to 200°C. Set the time to 20 minutes.
3. Press the START/STOP button to begin cooking.
4. After 10 minutes of cooking, open the air fryer and shake the basket to ensure even cooking. Close the air fryer and continue cooking for the remaining 10 minutes, or until the yam fries are golden brown and crispy.
5. Carefully remove the **yam fries** from the air fryer and transfer them to a serving dish.
6. Garnish with fresh chopped parsley and serve immediately.

Apple Turnovers

Prep: 15 Min | Cook: 15 Min | Serves: 6

Ingredient:

- 500g puff pastry, thawed
- 2 medium apples, peeled, cored, and diced
- 50g granulated sugar
- 1 teaspoon lemon juice
- 1/2 teaspoon ground cinnamon
- 1 tablespoon cornstarch
- 1 egg, beaten (for egg wash)
- Icing sugar (for dusting)

Instruction:

1. In a mixing bowl, combine the diced apples, granulated sugar, lemon juice, ground cinnamon, and cornstarch. Stir until the apples are evenly coated with the mixture.
2. Roll out the puff pastry on a lightly floured surface to a thickness of about 3-4mm. Cut the pastry into squares of approximately 12cm x 12cm.
3. Place a spoonful of the apple mixture onto the center of each pastry square.
4. Fold each pastry square diagonally to form a triangle, enclosing the apple filling. Press the edges firmly to seal.
5. Evenly dividing apple turnovers between the two zone in a single layer.
6. Select Zone 1, choose the BAKE program, and set the temperature to 180°C. Set the time to 12-15 minutes.
7. Brush the tops of the turnovers with beaten egg for a shiny finish.
8. Press the START/STOP button to begin cooking.
9. After 12-15 minutes, or until the turnovers are golden brown and crispy, carefully remove them from the air fryer.
10. Allow the turnovers to cool slightly before dusting them with icing sugar.
11. Serve the **apple turnovers** warm and enjoy!

CHAPTER 07: DESSERTS

Bakewell Tart Bites

Prep: 20 Min | Cook: 15 Min | Serves: 6 bites

Ingredient:

- 100g shortcrust pastry
- 50g unsalted butter, softened
- 50g granulated sugar
- 1 large egg
- 50g ground almonds
- 1/2 tsp almond extract
- 1 tbsp raspberry jam
- Flaked almonds, for garnish

Instruction:

1. Roll out the shortcrust pastry on a lightly floured surface. Using a round cookie cutter, cut out circles that will fit into the wells of a mini muffin tin.
2. Press the pastry circles into the wells of the mini muffin tin, making sure to press them up the sides.
3. In a mixing bowl, cream together the softened butter and granulated sugar until light and fluffy. Add the eggs, ground almonds, and almond extract to the bowl. Mix well to combine.
4. Spoon a small dollop of raspberry jam into the bottom of each pastry case.
5. Fill each pastry case with the almond mixture, covering the raspberry jam.
6. Sprinkle a few flaked almonds on top of each tart for garnish.
7. Place the mini muffin tin in Zone 1, leaving space between them for even cooking. Select Zone 1, choose the BAKE program, and set the temperature to 180°C. Set the time to 15 minutes.
8. Press the START/STOP.
9. After 10 minutes of air frying, carefully open the air fryer and check the tarts for doneness. They should be golden brown on top.
10. Once cooked, let them cool in the tin for a few minutes before transferring them to a wire rack to cool completely. Serve the **Bakewell Tart Bites** at room temperature as a delightful sweet treat.

Banana Fritters

Prep: 10 Min | Cook: 10 Min | Serves: 2-4

Ingredient:

- 2 ripe bananas
- 100g self-raising flour
- 50g granulated sugar
- 1/2 tsp ground cinnamon
- A pinch of salt
- 100ml milk
- Vegetable oil, for brushing
- Icing sugar, for dusting

Instruction:

1. In a mixing bowl, mash the ripe bananas with a fork until smooth.
2. Add the self-raising flour, granulated sugar, ground cinnamon, and a pinch of salt to the bowl. Mix well to combine.
3. Gradually pour in the milk while stirring, until a thick batter forms.
4. Brush the air fryer basket with a little vegetable oil to prevent sticking.
5. Drop spoonfuls of the banana batter into the air fryer basket, leaving some space between each fritter for even cooking.
6. Select Zone 1, choose the AIR FRY program, and set the temperature to 200°C. Set the time to 10 minutes.
7. Press the START/STOP button to begin air frying the Banana Fritters.
8. After 5 minutes of air frying, carefully open the air fryer and flip the fritters using tongs or a spatula. Brush the tops with a little more vegetable oil for a crispy texture.
9. Close the air fryer and continue cooking for the remaining 5 minutes.
10. Once the Banana Fritters are golden brown and crispy, carefully remove them from the air fryer and transfer them to a serving plate. Dust the **Banana Fritters** with icing sugar and serve them warm as a delightful dessert or snack.

CHAPTER 07: DESSERTS

Biscotti

Prep: 15 Min | Cook: 30 Min | Serves: 12 biscotti

Ingredient:

- 200g all-purpose flour
- 1 teaspoon baking powder
- 150g granulated sugar
- 2 large eggs
- 1 teaspoon vanilla extract
- 50g chopped almonds (or any other nuts of your choice)
- 50g dried cranberries (or any other dried fruit of your choice)

Instruction:

1. In a mixing bowl, whisk together the flour and baking powder.
2. In a separate bowl, beat the eggs, granulated sugar, and vanilla extract until well combined.
3. Gradually add the egg mixture to the flour mixture and mix until a dough forms.
4. Fold in the chopped almonds and dried cranberries until evenly distributed throughout the dough.
5. Divide the dough in half. On a lightly floured surface, shape each portion into a log about 3 cm wide and 1 cm thick.
6. Place logs between the two zones. Select Zone 1, choose the BAKE program, and set the temperature to 160°C. Set the time to 15 minutes to bake the logs. Select MATCH. Press the START/STOP button to begin cooking.
7. Once the logs are cool enough to handle, use a sharp knife to slice them diagonally into 1.5 cm thick slices.
8. Place the sliced biscotti in both zones. Select Zone 2, choose the AIR FRY program, and set the temperature to 160°C. Set the time to 15 minutes to bake the biscotti slices. Press the START/STOP.
9. After 15 minutes, check the biscotti for desired crispness. If they need more time, cook for an additional 5 minutes.
10. Once cooked, remove the **biscotti** from the air fryer and let them cool completely before serving or storing in an airtight container.

Blackberry Fool

Prep: 10 Min | Cook: 5 Min | Serves: 4

Ingredient:

- 500g fresh blackberries
- 100g granulated sugar
- 300ml double cream
- 1 tsp vanilla extract

▶ Instruction:

1. In a mixing bowl, combine the fresh blackberries and granulated sugar. Toss gently to coat the blackberries in sugar.
2. Place the blackberries in Zone 1, ensuring they are in a single layer. Select Zone 1 and choose the AIR FRY program. Set the temperature to 180°C and the time to 5 minutes. Press the START/STOP button to begin air frying the blackberries.
3. After 5 minutes, carefully open the air fryer and check the blackberries. They should be slightly softened and releasing their juices. Remove the blackberries from the air fryer and let them cool for a few minutes.
4. Using a fork or a blender, lightly crush the blackberries to release more juice and create a chunky texture.
5. In a separate mixing bowl, whip the double cream and vanilla extract until soft peaks form.
6. Gently fold in the crushed blackberries into the whipped cream, leaving some streaks for a marbled effect.
7. Divide the blackberry fool mixture into serving glasses or bowls.
8. Cover and refrigerate the blackberry fool for at least 2 hours to allow the flavors to meld and the dessert to chill.
9. Before serving, you can garnish with additional fresh blackberries if desired.
10. Enjoy the refreshing and creamy **Blackberry Fool**!

CHAPTER 07: DESSERTS

Blueberry Muffins

Prep: 15 Min | Cook: 12 Min | Serves: 12 muffins

Ingredient:

- 200g self-raising flour
- 100g granulated sugar
- 100g unsalted butter, melted
- 2 large eggs
- 120ml milk
- 1 tsp vanilla extract
- 150g fresh blueberries
- A pinch of salt

▶ Instruction:

1. In a mixing bowl, combine the self-raising flour, granulated sugar, and a pinch of salt.
2. In a separate bowl, whisk together the melted butter, eggs, milk, and vanilla extract.
3. Pour the wet ingredients into the dry ingredients and mix until just combined. Do not overmix.
4. Gently fold in the fresh blueberries, being careful not to crush them.
5. Line a muffin tin with paper liners and fill each liner with the muffin batter, about two-thirds full.
6. Evenly dividing muffin tin between the two zone, leaving space between the muffins for even cooking.
7. Select Zone 1, choose the BAKE program, and set the temperature to 180°C. Set the time to 12 minutes. Select MATCH.
8. Press the START/STOP button to begin air frying the muffins.
9. After 10 minutes of air frying, carefully open the air fryer and check the muffins for doneness. They should be golden brown on top and a toothpick inserted into the center should come out clean.
10. If needed, continue cooking for an additional 1-2 minutes until the muffins are fully cooked.
11. Once cooked, carefully remove the muffins from the air fryer and let them cool slightly in the muffin tin.
12. Transfer the **muffins** to a wire rack to cool completely before serving.

Bread Pudding

Prep: 10 Min | Cook: 25 Min | Serves: 4

Ingredient:

- 300g stale bread, cut into cubes
- 500ml whole milk
- 100g granulated sugar
- 2 large eggs
- 1 tsp vanilla extract
- 100g raisins or sultanas
- 1/2 tsp ground cinnamon
- A pinch of nutmeg
- Butter, for greasing

Instruction:

1. Grease a baking dish or oven-safe dish with butter, ensuring it fits in Zone 1 of the air fryer.
2. In a mixing bowl, combine the stale bread cubes, raisins or sultanas, ground cinnamon, and a pinch of nutmeg.
3. In a saucepan, heat the milk over medium heat until it just begins to simmer. Remove from heat.
4. In a separate mixing bowl, whisk together the granulated sugar, eggs, and vanilla extract until well combined. Slowly pour the warm milk into the egg mixture, whisking continuously to prevent curdling. Pour the milk and egg mixture over the bread cubes, ensuring all the bread cubes are soaked.
5. Let the mixture sit for about 10 minutes, allowing the bread to absorb the liquid.
6. Transfer the bread mixture to the greased baking dish, spreading it out evenly.
7. Place the baking dish in Zone 1. Select Zone 1, choose the BAKE program, and set the temperature to 180°C. Set the time to 25 minutes. Press the START/STOP.
8. After 25 minutes, carefully open the air fryer and check the bread pudding. It should be golden brown on top and set in the center.
9. Once cooked, let the bread pudding cool slightly before serving. Serve the warm **Bread Pudding** as is or with a drizzle of custard or a scoop of vanilla ice cream.

CHAPTER 07: DESSERTS

Carrot Cake Cupcakes

Prep: 15 Min | Cook: 15 Min

Serves: 6 cupcakes

Ingredient:

For the cupcakes:
- 75g self-raising flour
- 1/4 tsp baking powder
- 1/4 tsp ground cinnamon
- 1/8 tsp ground nutmeg
- 1/8 tsp ground ginger
- 1/8 tsp salt
- 75g light brown sugar
- 1 large egg
- 60ml vegetable oil
- 1/2 teaspoon vanilla extract
- 75g grated carrots
- 25g chopped walnuts (optional)

For the cream cheese frosting:
- 75g cream cheese
- 37g unsalted butter
- 150g icing sugar
- 1/2 tsp vanilla extract

Instruction:

1. In a mixing bowl, whisk together the self-raising flour, baking powder, ground cinnamon, ground nutmeg, ground ginger, and salt.
2. In a separate bowl, beat together the light brown sugar, egg, vegetable oil, and vanilla extract until well combined.
3. Gradually add the dry ingredients to the wet ingredients, mixing until just combined.
4. Fold in the grated carrots and chopped walnuts (if using).
5. Line a cupcake tin with paper liners. Scoop the cupcake batter into the liners, filling each one about 2/3 full.
6. Place the cupcake tin in Zone 1. Select Zone 1, choose the Bake program, and set the temperature to 170°C. Set the time to 15-18 minutes to bake the cupcakes. Press the START/STOP.
7. After 15-18 minutes, carefully remove the cupcakes from the air fryer and let them cool completely on a wire rack.
8. While the cupcakes are cooling, prepare the cream cheese frosting. In a mixing bowl, beat together the softened cream cheese, softened unsalted butter, icing sugar, and vanilla extract until smooth and creamy.
9. Once the cupcakes are completely cooled, pipe or spread the cream cheese frosting on top of each cupcake.
10. Optional: Garnish with additional grated carrots or chopped walnuts for decoration. Serve and enjoy your homemade **Carrot Cake Cupcakes**!

Chocolate Brownies

Prep: 15 Min | Cook: 20 Min | Serves: 12 brownies

Ingredient:

- 200g unsalted butter
- 200g dark chocolate, chopped
- 250g granulated sugar
- 3 large eggs
- 1 tsp vanilla extract
- 100g self-raising flour
- 25g cocoa powder
- A pinch of salt

▶ Instruction:

1. In a microwave-safe bowl, melt the unsalted butter and dark chocolate together. Stir until smooth.
2. In a separate mixing bowl, whisk together the granulated sugar, eggs, and vanilla extract until well combined.
3. Pour the melted chocolate mixture into the sugar and egg mixture. Stir until fully incorporated.
4. Sift the self-raising flour, cocoa powder, and salt into the chocolate mixture. Gently fold until just combined.
5. Grease a baking dish or oven-safe dish that fits in Zone 1.
6. Pour the brownie batter into the greased baking dish, spreading it out evenly.
7. Place the baking dish in Zone 1. Select Zone 1, choose the AIR FRY program, and set the temperature to 180°C. Set the time to 20 minutes. Press the START/STOP.
8. After 20 minutes, carefully open the air fryer and check the brownies. They should be slightly crispy on top and a toothpick inserted into the center should have a few crumbs.
9. If needed, continue cooking for an additional 1-2 minutes until the brownies are fully cooked.
10. Once cooked, let the brownies cool completely before slicing.
11. Slice into 12 squares and serve these indulgent **Chocolate Brownies**!

CHAPTER 07: DESSERTS

Chocolate Chip Cookies

Prep: 15 Min | Cook: 10 Min | Serves: 12 cookies

Ingredient:

- 125g unsalted butter, softened
- 100g granulated sugar
- 100g light brown sugar
- 1 teaspoon vanilla extract
- 1 large egg
- 225g all-purpose flour
- 1/2 teaspoon baking soda
- 1/4 teaspoon salt
- 150g chocolate chips

▶ Instruction:

1. In a large mixing bowl, cream together the softened butter, light brown sugar, and granulated sugar until light and fluffy.
2. Add the egg and vanilla extract to the bowl. Mix well until combined.
3. In a separate bowl, whisk together the all-purpose flour, baking soda, and salt.
4. Gradually add the dry ingredients to the wet ingredients, mixing until just combined.
5. Fold in the chocolate chips until evenly distributed throughout the dough.
6. Scoop out tablespoon-sized portion of dough and roll it into balls. Evenly dividing cookies between the two zone, ensuring they are in a single layer.
7. Select Zone 1, choose the AIR FRY program, and set the temperature to 175°C. Set the time to 8-10 minutes. Select MATCH to duplicate settings across both zones. Press the START/STOP button to begin cooking.
8. Check the cookies after 8 minutes to see if they are golden brown. If needed, cook for an additional 1-2 minutes.
9. Once cooked, carefully remove the cookies from the air fryer and let them cool on a wire rack.
10. Enjoy the freshly baked **chocolate chip cookies**!

Chocolate Lava Cake

Prep: 15 Min | Cook: 8 Min

Serves: 4 lava cakes

Ingredient:

- 100g unsalted butter, plus extra for greasing
- 100g dark chocolate, chopped
- 2 large eggs
- 2 large egg yolks
- 75g granulated sugar
- 1 tsp vanilla extract
- 40g plain flour
- A pinch of salt
- Icing sugar, for dusting

Instruction:

1. Grease 4 ramekins in Zone 1 of the air fryer with butter.
2. In a microwave-safe bowl, melt the unsalted butter and dark chocolate together. Stir until smooth.
3. In a separate mixing bowl, whisk together the eggs, egg yolks, granulated sugar, and vanilla extract until well combined.
4. Pour the melted chocolate mixture into the egg mixture. Whisk until fully incorporated.
5. Sift the plain flour and salt into the chocolate mixture. Gently fold until just combined.
6. Divide the batter equally among the greased ramekins, filling them about three-fourths full.
7. Place the ramekins in Zone 1. Select Zone 1, choose the AIR FRY program, and set the temperature to 200°C. Set the time to 8 minutes. Press the START/STOP.
8. After 8 minutes, carefully open the air fryer and check the lava cakes. They should be set around the edges and slightly jiggly in the center.
9. Once cooked, let the lava cakes cool for a few minutes.
10. Run a knife around the edges of each ramekin and invert the lava cakes onto serving plates.
11. Dust with icing sugar and serve immediately, allowing the warm **chocolate** center to ooze out.

CHAPTER 07: DESSERTS

Churros

Prep: 15 Min | Cook: 10 Min | Serves: 4

Ingredient:

- 200g plain flour
- 1 teaspoon baking powder
- 1/2 teaspoon salt
- 250ml water
- 50g unsalted butter
- 2 tablespoons granulated sugar
- 1 teaspoon vanilla extract
- Vegetable oil, for greasing
- 50g granulated sugar, for coating
- 1 teaspoon ground cinnamon, for coating

Instruction:

1. In a medium-sized bowl, whisk together the plain flour, baking powder, and salt.
2. In a saucepan, combine the water, unsalted butter, granulated sugar, and vanilla extract. Bring the mixture to a boil over medium heat. Remove the saucepan from the heat and gradually add the flour mixture to the saucepan. Stir vigorously until a smooth dough forms. Transfer the dough to a piping bag fitted with a star-shaped nozzle.
3. Lightly grease the air fryer basket with vegetable oil.
4. Pipe the dough directly into the air fryer basket, forming long churro shapes, about 12 cm in length. Evenly dividing churros between the two zone, Leave some space between the churros. Select Zone 1, choose the AIR FRY program, and set the temperature to 190°C. Set the time to 10 minutes to cook the churros. Select MATCH. Press the START/STOP.
5. While the churros are cooking, combine the granulated sugar and ground cinnamon in a shallow bowl.
6. Once the churros are cooked, carefully remove them from the air fryer and let them cool for a few seconds.
7. While the churros are still warm, roll them in the cinnamon sugar mixture until coated.
8. Serve the **churros** immediately, optionally with chocolate sauce or caramel sauce for dipping.

Cinnamon Rolls

Prep: 10 Min | Cook: 5 Min | Serves: 4

Ingredient:

For the dough:
- 300g all-purpose flour
- 50g granulated sugar
- 1 teaspoon instant yeast
- 1/2 teaspoon salt
- 150ml warm milk
- 40g unsalted butter, melted
- 1 large egg

For the filling:
- 50g unsalted butter, softened
- 50g light brown sugar
- 1 tablespoon ground cinnamon

For the glaze:
- 100g icing sugar
- 1-2 tablespoons milk
- 1/2 teaspoon vanilla extract

➤ Instruction:

1. In a large mixing bowl, combine the flour, granulated sugar, instant yeast, and salt.
2. In a separate bowl, whisk together the warm milk, melted butter, and egg. Pour the wet ingredients into the dry ingredients and mix until a dough forms.
3. Turn the dough out onto a lightly floured surface and knead for about 5 minutes, or until smooth and elastic.
4. Using a rolling pin, roll out the dough into a rectangle about 20 cm x 25 cm. Spread the softened butter evenly over the dough.
5. In a small bowl, mix together the brown sugar and ground cinnamon. Sprinkle the mixture evenly over the buttered dough.
6. Starting from one of the longer sides, tightly roll up the dough into a log.
7. Cut the log into 8 equal-sized pieces. Evenly dividing cinnamon rolls between the two zone, leaving some space between them. Select Zone 1, choose the AIR FRY program, and set the temperature to 180°C. Set the time to 12 minutes to bake the cinnamon rolls. Select MATCH. Press the START/STOP.
8. While the cinnamon rolls are baking, prepare the glaze. In a small bowl, whisk together the icing sugar, milk, and vanilla extract until smooth and pourable.
9. Drizzle the glaze over the warm cinnamon rolls. Serve the **Cinnamon Rolls** immediately and enjoy!

CHAPTER 07: DESSERTS

Lemon Bars

Prep: 15 Min | Cook: 25 Min

Serves: 12 lemon bars

Ingredient:

For the crust:
- 200g plain flour
- 50g icing sugar
- 120g unsalted butter, cold and cubed

For the filling:
- 4 large eggs
- 200g granulated sugar
- 3 tbsp plain flour
- Zest of 2 lemons
- Juice of 3 lemons

➤ Instruction:

1. In a food processor, combine the plain flour, icing sugar, and cold cubed unsalted butter. Pulse until the mixture resembles fine breadcrumbs.
2. Grease a baking dish that fits in Zone 1, or line it with parchment paper. Transfer the crust mixture to the prepared baking dish and press it down evenly to form the crust.
3. Place the baking dish in Zone . Select Zone 1, choose the AIR FRY program, and set the temperature to 180°C. Set the time to 8-10 minutes for pre-baking the crust. Press the START/STOP button to begin air frying the crust.
4. After 8-10 minutes, carefully open the air fryer and check the crust. It should be lightly golden brown. Remove the pre-baked crust from the air fryer and set it aside to cool.
5. In a mixing bowl, whisk together the eggs, granulated sugar, plain flour, lemon zest, and lemon juice until well combined.
6. Pour the lemon filling over the cooled crust, spreading it evenly.
7. Place the baking dish back in Zone 1. Select Zone 1, choose the AIR FRY program, and set the temperature to 180°C. Set the time to 12-15 minutes. Press the START/STOP.
8. After 12-15 minutes, carefully open the air fryer and check the lemon bars. The filling should be set and slightly firm to the touch.
9. Once cooked, let the lemon bars cool completely. Cut the **lemon bars** into squares or rectangles and dust with icing sugar before serving.

Lemon Drizzle Cake

Prep: 15 Min | Cook: 30 Min

Serves: 8-10 slices

Ingredient:

For the cake:
- 200g unsalted butter, softened
- 200g caster sugar
- 4 large eggs
- 200g self-raising flour
- Zest of 2 lemons

For the drizzle:
- Juice of 2 lemons
- 100g granulated sugar
- For the icing (optional):
- 100g icing sugar
- Juice of 1 lemon

➤ Instruction:

1. In a mixing bowl, cream together the softened unsalted butter and caster sugar until light and fluffy.
2. Add the eggs, one at a time, beating well after each addition.
3. Sift the self-raising flour into the bowl and fold it into the mixture until fully incorporated. Stir in the lemon zest.
4. Grease a cake tin or line it with parchment paper. The cake tin should fit in Zone 1. Pour the cake batter into the prepared tin, spreading it out evenly.
5. Place the cake tin in Zone 1. Select Zone 1, choose the BAKE program, set temperature to 160°C, set time to 25-30 minutes for baking the cake. Press the START/STOP.
6. After 25-30 minutes, check the cake; it should be golden brown, and a skewer inserted into the center should come out clean.
7. While the cake is still warm in the tin, prepare the lemon drizzle by mixing the lemon juice and granulated sugar together until the sugar dissolves. Use a skewer to poke holes all over the surface of the warm cake, then pour the lemon drizzle over it, ensuring it seeps into the holes.
8. Let the cake cool completely in the tin before removing it. If desired, prepare the icing by mixing the icing sugar and lemon juice until smooth. Drizzle the icing over the cooled cake. Slice and serve the **Lemon Drizzle Cake**, enjoying its tangy and moist texture.

CHAPTER 07: DESSERTS

Lemon Meringue Pie

Prep: 20 Min | Cook: 18 Min

Serves: 8 slices

Ingredient:

For the crust:
- 200g digestive biscuits, crushed
- 100g unsalted butter, melted

For the filling:
- 4 large egg yolks
- 400g can condensed milk
- Zest of 2 lemons
- Juice of 3 lemons

For the meringue:
- 4 large egg whites
- 200g caster sugar

➤ Instruction:

1. In a mixing bowl, combine the crushed digestive biscuits and melted unsalted butter. Mix well until the crumbs are evenly coated. Grease a pie dish that fits in Zone 1. Press the biscuit mixture evenly onto the bottom and sides of the pie dish to form the crust.
2. Place the pie dish in Zone 1. Select Zone 1, choose the AIR FRY program, set temperature to 180°C, set the time to 6-8 minutes. Press the START/STOP.
3. After 6-8 minutes, carefully open the air fryer and check the crust. Remove the crust from the air fryer and let it cool completely.
4. In a separate bowl, whisk together the egg yolks, condensed milk, lemon zest, and lemon juice until well combined. Pour the lemon filling into the cooled crust, spreading it out evenly.
5. Place the pie dish back in Zone 1. Choose the AIR FRY program, set the temperature to 180°C, set time to 8-10 minutes. After 8-10 minutes, check the lemon filling.
6. While the pie is cooling, prepare the meringue by whisking the egg whites until stiff peaks form. Gradually add the caster sugar, whisking continuously, until the meringue is glossy and thick. Spread the meringue over the cooled lemon filling, ensuring it reaches the edges and forms peaks.
7. Place the pie dish back in Zone 1. Choose the AIR FRY program, temperature to 160°C, time to 5-6 minutes. After 5-6 minutes, check the meringue. Remove the **pie** from the air fryer and let it cool completely before slicing and serving.

Mini Fruit Pies

Prep: 30 Min | Cook: 15 Min

Serves: 6 mini fruit pies

Ingredient:

For the pastry:
- 250g plain flour
- 125g unsalted butter, cold and cubed
- 50g icing sugar
- 1 large egg, beaten

For the fruit filling:
- 300g mixed fresh fruit (such as berries, peaches, or apples), chopped
- 50g granulated sugar
- 1 tbsp cornstarch
- 1 tsp lemon juice

Instruction:

1. In a food processor, combine the plain flour, cold cubed unsalted butter, and icing sugar. Pulse until the mixture resembles fine breadcrumbs. Add the beaten egg and pulse again until the dough comes together. Transfer the pastry dough to a floured surface and knead it gently until smooth. Wrap the pastry in cling film and refrigerate for 15 minutes.
2. Prepare the fruit filling by combining the mixed fresh fruit, granulated sugar, cornstarch, and lemon juice in a bowl. Toss until the fruit is coated. Grease individual pie tins or use silicone baking molds. Roll out the chilled pastry dough on a floured surface to about 3mm thickness. Cut out rounds of pastry slightly larger than the pie tins or molds.
3. Line each tin or mold with a pastry round, pressing it into the bottom and sides. Fill with the fruit filling. Cut out smaller rounds or strips of pastry for a lattice or decorative top.
4. Place the pies in Zone 1. Select Zone 1, choose the BAKE program, and set the temperature to 180°C for 12-15 minutes. Press START/STOP.
5. After 12-15 minutes, check the pies. The pastry should be golden brown and the fruit filling bubbling.
6. Once cooked, remove the pie tins or molds from the air fryer and let the **mini fruit pies** cool slightly before serving.

CHAPTER 07: DESSERTS

Mint Aero Tartlets

Prep: 20 Min | Cook: 10 Min | Serves: 6 tartlets

Ingredient:

- 200g digestive biscuits
- 100g unsalted butter, melted
- 200g dark chocolate
- 200ml double cream
- 1 teaspoon peppermint extract
- Green food coloring (optional)
- Mint Aero chocolate bars, for garnish

Instruction:

1. Place the digestive biscuits in a resealable bag and crush them using a rolling pin until they resemble fine crumbs.
2. In a bowl, mix the crushed biscuits with the melted butter until well combined.
3. Divide the biscuit mixture evenly among six individual tartlet tins. Press the mixture firmly into the bottom and sides of each tin to form the tartlet crusts.
4. Place the tartlet tins in two zones. Select Zone 1, choose the BAKE program, and set the time to 10 minutes at 180°C. Select MATCH. Press the START/STOP.
5. Break the dark chocolate into pieces and place it in a heatproof bowl.
6. In a small saucepan, heat the double cream until it just starts to bubble around the edges. Remove from heat. Pour the hot cream over the dark chocolate and let it sit for a minute. Stir the chocolate and cream mixture until smooth and glossy.
7. Once the tartlet crusts are cooked and golden brown, carefully remove the tartlet tins from the Air Fryer and let them cool for a few minutes. Pour the mint chocolate mixture into each tartlet crust, dividing it evenly among the tins.
8. Place the tartlet tins in the refrigerator to set for at least 2 hours, or until the filling is firm.
9. Before serving, garnish each tartlet with pieces of Mint Aero chocolate bars. Serve the **Mint Aero Tartlets** chilled.

Peach Cobbler

Prep: 15 Min | Cook: 20 Min | Serves: 4-6

Ingredient:

- 500g fresh or canned peaches, sliced
- 100g granulated sugar
- 1 tablespoon lemon juice
- 1 teaspoon vanilla extract
- 100g self-raising flour
- 50g unsalted butter, melted
- 100ml milk
- 1/2 teaspoon ground cinnamon
- A pinch of salt
- Vanilla ice cream or whipped cream, for serving (optional)

▶ Instruction:

1. In a mixing bowl, combine the sliced peaches, granulated sugar, lemon juice, and vanilla extract. Stir until the peaches are coated in the sugar mixture. Let it sit for about 10 minutes to allow the flavors to meld.
2. In another bowl, mix together the self-raising flour, melted butter, milk, ground cinnamon, and salt until well combined.
3. Grease a small baking dish that fits inside the air fryer basket.
4. Pour the peach mixture into the greased baking dish, spreading it out evenly.
5. Pour the batter mixture over the peaches, covering them completely.
6. In Zone 1, place the baking dish in the basket. Select Zone 1, choose the BAKE program, and set the temperature to 180°C. Set the time to 20 minutes. Press the START/STOP button to begin cooking.
7. After 20 minutes, carefully remove the baking dish from the air fryer.
8. Allow the peach cobbler to cool slightly before serving.
9. Serve the **peach cobbler** warm, topped with a scoop of vanilla ice cream or whipped cream if desired.

CHAPTER 07: DESSERTS

Pear Tart

Prep: 20 Min | Cook: 25 Min | Serves: 6-8

Ingredient:

For the crust:
- 200g plain flour
- 100g unsalted butter, cold and cubed
- 50g icing sugar
- 1 large egg yolk

For the filling:
- 3 ripe pears, peeled, cored, and thinly sliced
- 50g granulated sugar
- 1 tablespoon lemon juice
- 1 teaspoon ground cinnamon

For the glaze:
- 2 tablespoons apricot jam
- 1 tablespoon water

▶ Instruction:

1. In a food processor, combine the plain flour, cubed butter, and icing sugar. Pulse until the mixture resembles coarse crumbs.
2. Add the egg yolk and pulse until the dough comes together.
3. Turn the dough out onto a lightly floured surface and knead it briefly until smooth.
4. Roll out the dough into a circle about 20 cm in diameter.
5. Carefully transfer the rolled-out dough to a tart pan, pressing it into the bottom and up the sides. Trim off any excess dough.
6. In a bowl, combine the sliced pears, granulated sugar, lemon juice, and ground cinnamon. Toss to coat the pears evenly.
7. Arrange the pear slices in a single layer over the tart crust, slightly overlapping them.
8. Place the tart in Zone 1. Select Zone 1, choose the BAKE program, and set the temperature to 180°C. Set the time to 25 minutes to bake the tart. Press the START/STOP.
9. While the tart is baking, prepare the glaze. In a small saucepan, heat the apricot jam and water over low heat until melted and smooth.
10. After 25 minutes, carefully remove the tart from the air fryer and let it cool for a few minutes.
11. Brush the warm tart with the apricot glaze, ensuring to coat the pear slices and the crust.
12. Allow the **tart** to cool completely before serving.

Pumpkin Pie

Prep: 30 Min | Cook: 30 Min | Serves: 4

Ingredient:

For the crust:
- 200g plain flour
- 100g unsalted butter, cold and cubed
- 1 tbsp granulated sugar
- Pinch of salt
- 2-3 tbsp cold water

For the filling:
- 400g canned pumpkin puree
- 200g condensed milk
- 2 large eggs
- 1 tsp ground cinnamon
- 1/2 tsp ground ginger
- 1/4 tsp ground nutmeg
- 1/4 tsp ground cloves
- Pinch of salt

Instruction:

1. In a mixing bowl, combine the plain flour, cold cubed unsalted butter, granulated sugar, and salt. Rub the butter into the flour mixture with your fingertips until it resembles breadcrumbs.
2. Gradually add the cold water, a tablespoon at a time, and mix until the dough comes together. Transfer the dough to a floured surface and knead it gently until smooth. Wrap the pastry in cling film and refrigerate for 15 minutes.
3. In the meantime, prepare the pumpkin filling by whisking together the canned pumpkin puree, condensed milk, eggs, ground cinnamon, ground ginger, ground nutmeg, ground cloves, and salt in a bowl until well combined.
4. Grease a pie dish that fits in Zone 1, or use a silicone baking mat that fits in the dish. Take the chilled pastry dough and roll it out on a floured surface to fit the pie dish. Line the pie dish with the rolled-out pastry, pressing it gently into the bottom and sides. Pour the pumpkin filling into the pastry-lined dish, spreading it out evenly.
5. Place the pie dish in Zone 1. Select Zone 1, choose the BAKE program, and set the temperature to 180°C. Set the time to 25-30 minutes for baking the pumpkin pie. Press the START/STOP.
6. After 25-30 minutes, carefully open the air fryer and check the **pumpkin pie**. The filling should be set and slightly firm to the touch. Remove the pie from the air fryer and let it cool completely before slicing and serving.

CHAPTER 07: DESSERTS

Raspberry Bakewell Tarts

Prep: 20 Min | Cook: 20 Min | Serves: 6-8

Ingredient:

For the Pastry:
- 200g plain flour
- 100g unsalted butter, cold and cubed
- 2 tablespoons icing sugar
- 1 large egg yolk
- 2-3 tablespoons cold water

For the Filling:
- 150g raspberry jam
- 150g ground almonds
- 100g unsalted butter, softened
- 100g caster sugar
- 2 large eggs
- 1 teaspoon almond extract
- Handful of flaked almonds, for topping

Instruction:

1. In a mixing bowl, combine the flour and cold, cubed butter. Rub the butter into the flour using your fingertips until the mixture resembles breadcrumbs. Stir in the icing sugar. Then add the egg yolk and 2-3 tablespoons of cold water. Mix until the dough comes together. Add more water if needed. Transfer the dough onto a lightly floured surface and knead it briefly until smooth. Shape it into a disc, cover with plastic wrap, and refrigerate for 15 minutes.
2. In the meantime, prepare the filling. In a bowl, mix together the ground almonds, softened butter, caster sugar, eggs, and almond extract until well combined. On a lightly floured surface, roll out the chilled pastry to a thickness of about 3mm. Cut out circles of pastry using a round cutter that fits the size of your tart molds or a glass.
3. Grease the tart molds and line them with the pastry circles, gently pressing them into the bottom and sides.
4. Spread a teaspoon of raspberry jam onto the bottom of each pastry case. Spoon the almond filling on top of the jam, filling each case to about two-thirds full. Sprinkle flaked almonds on top of each tart.
5. In Zone 1, place the tart molds in the basket. Select Zone 1, choose the BAKE program, and set the temperature to 180°C. Set the time to 20 minutes. Press the START/STOP.
6. After 20 minutes, carefully remove the tart molds from the air fryer and let them cool slightly. Once cooled, remove the **tarts** from the molds and place them on a wire rack to cool completely.

Rhubarb Crisp

Prep: 15 Min | Cook: 25 Min | Serves: 4-6

Ingredient:

For the Filling:
- 500g rhubarb stalks, trimmed and cut into 2cm pieces
- 100g granulated sugar
- 1 tablespoon cornstarch
- 1/2 teaspoon ground cinnamon
- 1/4 teaspoon ground ginger
- Zest of 1 orange

For the Topping:
- 100g plain flour
- 50g rolled oats
- 50g light brown sugar
- 50g unsalted butter, cold and cubed

Instruction:

1. In a mixing bowl, combine the rhubarb pieces, granulated sugar, cornstarch, ground cinnamon, ground ginger, and orange zest. Toss until the rhubarb is evenly coated with the mixture.
2. In a separate bowl, mix together the plain flour, rolled oats, light brown sugar, and cold, cubed butter. Use your fingertips to rub the butter into the dry ingredients until the mixture resembles coarse crumbs.
3. Grease a baking dish that fits inside the air fryer basket.
4. Transfer the rhubarb filling into the greased baking dish, spreading it out evenly.
5. Sprinkle the topping mixture over the rhubarb, covering it completely.
6. In Zone 1 of the air fryer, place the baking dish in the basket. Select Zone 1, choose the BAKE program, and set the temperature to 180°C. Set the time to 20-25 minutes.
7. Press the START/STOP button to begin cooking.
8. After 20-25 minutes, carefully remove the baking dish from the air fryer.
9. Allow the rhubarb crisp to cool slightly before serving.
10. Serve the **rhubarb crisp** warm, either on its own or with a scoop of vanilla ice cream or whipped cream if desired.

CHAPTER 07: DESSERTS

Sticky Toffee Pudding

Prep: 20 Min | Cook: 30 Min | Serves: 6-8

Ingredient:

For the Cake:
- 200g pitted dates, roughly chopped
- 200ml boiling water
- 1 teaspoon bicarbonate of soda
- 100g unsalted butter, softened
- 175g light brown sugar
- 2 large eggs
- 200g self-raising flour

For the Toffee Sauce:
- 200g light brown sugar
- 200ml double cream
- 50g unsalted butter

Instruction:

1. In a heatproof bowl, combine the chopped dates and boiling water. Stir in the bicarbonate of soda and let it sit for 10 minutes to soften the dates.
2. In the meantime, in a mixing bowl, cream together the softened butter and light brown sugar until light and fluffy. Beat in the eggs, one at a time, until well combined. Gradually fold in the self-raising flour until the batter is smooth. Add the softened dates along with any remaining liquid to the batter. Mix until well combined.
3. Grease a baking dish that fits inside the air fryer basket. Transfer the batter into the greased baking dish, spreading it out evenly.
4. In Zone 1, place the baking dish in the basket. Select Zone 1, choose the BAKE program, and set the temperature to 180°C. Set the time to 25-30 minutes. Press the START/STOP.
5. While the cake is baking, prepare the toffee sauce. In a saucepan, combine the light brown sugar, double cream, and unsalted butter. Heat over medium heat, stirring constantly, until the sugar has dissolved and the mixture is smooth and thickened.
6. Once the cake is done, carefully remove the baking dish from the air fryer.
7. Poke several holes in the top of the cake using a skewer.
8. Pour about two-thirds of the toffee sauce over the warm cake, allowing it to soak into the holes. Serve the **sticky toffee pudding** warm, drizzled with the remaining toffee sauce.

Stuffed Dates

Prep: 10 Min | Cook: 5 Min | Serves: 6

Ingredient:

- 150g Medjool dates, pitted
- 75g soft goat cheese
- 25g walnuts, chopped
- 1 tablespoon honey
- Zest of 1 orange

▶ Instruction:

1. In a small bowl, mix together the soft goat cheese, chopped walnuts, honey, and orange zest until well combined.
2. Take each pitted date and gently open it up to create a pocket.
3. Spoon a small amount of the goat cheese mixture into each date, filling it up without overstuffing.
4. Press the sides of the date together to seal the filling.
5. Grease the air fryer basket to prevent sticking.
6. In Zone 1 of the air fryer, place the stuffed dates in the basket. Select Zone 1, choose the AIR FRY program, and set the temperature to 180°C. Set the time to 5 minutes.
7. Press the START/STOP button to begin cooking.
8. After 5 minutes, carefully remove the stuffed dates from the air fryer.
9. Allow the **stuffed dates** to cool slightly before serving.
10. Serve the stuffed dates as a delicious sweet treat or appetizer.

CHAPTER 07: DESSERTS

Treacle Tart

Prep: 20 Min | Cook: 20 Min | Serves: 6

Ingredient:

- 250g plain flour
- 125g unsalted butter, cold and cubed
- 50g golden syrup
- 50g black treacle
- 1 large lemon, zested and juiced
- 100g fresh breadcrumbs
- 1 egg, beaten

▶ Instruction:

1. In a mixing bowl, combine the plain flour and cold cubed unsalted butter.
2. Rub the butter into the flour with your fingertips until it resembles breadcrumbs. Add the golden syrup, black treacle, lemon zest, and lemon juice to the flour mixture. Mix until well combined. Transfer the mixture to a food processor and pulse a few times to form a dough. Wrap the dough in cling film and refrigerate for 15 minutes.
3. In the meantime, prepare the filling by combining the fresh breadcrumbs and beaten egg in a bowl. Mix until the breadcrumbs are coated. Grease a pie dish that fits in Zone 1, or use a silicone baking mat that fits in the dish. Take the chilled dough and roll it out on a floured surface to fit the pie dish.
4. Line the pie dish with the rolled-out dough, pressing it gently into the bottom and sides.
5. Spread the breadcrumb mixture evenly over the pastry base.
6. Place the pie dish in Zone 1 of the Ninja Dual Zone Air Fryer.
7. Select Zone 1, choose the BAKE program, and set the temperature to 180°C. Set the time to 15-20 minutes for baking the treacle tart. Press the START/STOP.
8. After 15-20 minutes, carefully open the air fryer and check the treacle tart. The pastry should be golden brown and the filling should be set. Remove the **Treacle Tart** from the air fryer and let it cool slightly before serving.

Aubergine Parmesan

Prep: 20 Min | Cook: 30 Min | Serves: 4

Ingredient:

- 2 large aubergines (eggplants)
- 200g breadcrumbs
- 100g vegan Parmesan-style cheese, grated
- 500g tomato passata (pureed tomatoes)
- 2 garlic cloves, minced
- 1 teaspoon dried oregano
- Salt, to taste
- Pepper, to taste
- Fresh basil leaves, for garnish

➤ Instruction:

1. Slice the aubergines into 1 cm thick rounds.
2. In a shallow bowl, combine the breadcrumbs and grated vegan Parmesan-style cheese. Dip each aubergine slice into the breadcrumb mixture, pressing lightly to adhere the coating.
3. Place the breaded aubergine slices in Zone 1 of the air fryer basket, making sure they are in a single layer.
4. Select Zone 1 and choose the AIR FRY program. Set the temperature to 200°C for 15 minutes. Press the START/STOP.
5. After 8 minutes of cooking, open the air fryer and flip the aubergine slices to ensure even browning. Once the cooking is complete, remove the aubergine slices from Zone 1 and set them aside.
6. In a saucepan, heat the tomato passata over medium heat. Add the minced garlic, dried oregano, salt, and pepper. Simmer for 5 minutes, stirring occasionally.
7. To assemble, place a layer of the cooked aubergine slices in a baking dish. Top with a layer of tomato sauce. Repeat the layers, finishing with a layer of tomato sauce on top.
8. Place the assembled dish in the Zone 1 of the air fryer.
9. Select Zone 1 and choose BAKE program. Set the temperature to 180°C for 15 minutes. Press the START/STOP.
10. Serve the **Aubergine Parmesan** warm as a delicious and satisfying main dish.

CHAPTER 08: VEGETARIAN

Butternut Squash Fries

Prep: 10 Min | Cook: 20 Min | Serves: 4

Ingredient:

- 1 medium butternut squash (about 800g)
- 2 tablespoons olive oil
- 1 teaspoon paprika
- 1/2 teaspoon garlic powder
- 1/2 teaspoon salt
- 1/4 teaspoon black pepper
- Fresh parsley, for garnish

➤ Instruction:

1. Peel the butternut squash and cut it into 1 cm thick fries, approximately 7 cm long.
2. In a mixing bowl, combine the olive oil, paprika, garlic powder, salt, and black pepper. Mix well.
3. Place the butternut squash fries in Zone 1 of the air fryer basket.
4. Drizzle the seasoned oil mixture over the fries, ensuring they are well coated.
5. Select Zone 1 and choose the AIR FRY program. Set the temperature to 200°C and the time to 20 minutes. Press the START/STOP button to begin cooking the fries.
6. After 10 minutes of cooking, open the air fryer and shake the basket to flip the fries for even cooking.
7. Close the air fryer and continue cooking for the remaining 10 minutes, or until the fries are golden brown and crispy.
8. Once the cooking is complete, remove the butternut squash fries from Zone 1 and let them cool for a few minutes.
9. Garnish with fresh parsley.
10. Serve the **Butternut Squash Fries** warm as a healthy and flavorful side dish, ideal for dipping in your favorite vegan sauces.

Cauliflower Wings

Prep: 15 Min | Cook: 30 Min | Serves: 4

Ingredient:

- 1 large cauliflower head (about 800g)
- 150g plain flour
- 200ml plant-based milk (such as almond or soy milk)
- 1 teaspoon garlic powder
- 1 teaspoon paprika
- 1/2 teaspoon salt
- 1/4 teaspoon black pepper
- 100g bread crumbs
- 100g vegan-friendly buffalo sauce or barbecue sauce
- Fresh parsley, for garnish

Instruction:

1. Cut the cauliflower into bite-sized florets.
2. In a mixing bowl, combine the plain flour, plant-based milk, garlic powder, paprika, salt, and black pepper to form a smooth batter.
3. Dip each cauliflower floret into the batter, ensuring it is fully coated. Roll the battered floret in the bread crumbs, pressing lightly to adhere the coating.
4. Place the breaded cauliflower wings in Zone 1 of the air fryer basket.
5. Select Zone 1 and the AIR FRY program. Set the temperature to 200°C for 25 minutes. Press the START/STOP.
6. After 15 minutes of cooking, open the air fryer and flip the cauliflower wings for even browning.
7. Once the cooking is complete, remove the cauliflower wings from Zone 1 and place them in a mixing bowl.
8. Pour the vegan-friendly buffalo sauce or barbecue sauce over the cauliflower wings and toss to coat evenly.
9. Return the sauced cauliflower wings to Zone 1 of the air fryer.
10. Select Zone 1 and the AIR FRY program. Set the temperature to 200°C for 5 minutes. Press the START/STOP.
11. Serve the **Cauliflower Wings** warm as a delicious and satisfying appetizer or snack, perfect for dipping in vegan-friendly sauces.

CHAPTER 08: VEGETARIAN

Cheesy Garlic Bread

Prep: 10 Min | Cook: 15 Min | Serves: 4

Ingredient:

- 1 large baguette (about 300g)
- 100g vegan butter, softened
- 3 cloves of garlic, minced
- 1 tablespoon fresh parsley, finely chopped
- 100g vegan cheese, grated (such as Violife or Sheese)
- Salt, to taste
- Fresh parsley, for garnish

Instruction:

1. Cut the baguette into diagonal slices, approximately 2 cm thick.
2. In a small bowl, combine the softened vegan butter, minced garlic, fresh parsley, and a pinch of salt. Mix well to create a garlic butter spread.
3. Spread the garlic butter mixture on one side of each baguette slice.
4. Place the baguette slices, buttered side up, in Zone 1 of the air fryer basket.
5. Sprinkle the grated vegan cheese evenly over the baguette slices.
6. Select Zone 1 and the AIR FRY program. Set the temperature to 180°C and the time to 15 minutes. Press the START/STOP button to begin cooking.
7. After 10 minutes of cooking, open the air fryer and check the bread for desired crispness and cheese melt. If needed, continue cooking for an additional 2-3 minutes.
8. Once the cooking is complete, remove the cheesy garlic bread from Zone 1. Garnish with fresh parsley.
9. Serve the **Cheesy Garlic Bread** warm as a delightful appetizer or side dish, perfect for sharing with friends and family.

Corn on the Cob

Prep: 5 Min | Cook: 15 Min | Serves: 4

Ingredient:

- 4 corn cobs
- 40g vegan butter, melted
- 1 teaspoon paprika
- 1/2 teaspoon garlic powder
- Salt, to taste
- Fresh parsley, for garnish

Instruction:

1. Remove the husks and silk from the corn cobs, ensuring they are clean and ready for cooking.
2. In a small bowl, combine the melted vegan butter, paprika, garlic powder, and a pinch of salt. Mix well to create a flavored butter mixture.
3. Brush the flavored butter mixture evenly over each corn cob, coating all sides.
4. Place the corn cobs in Zone 1 of the air fryer basket.
5. Select Zone 1 and the AIR FRY program. Set the temperature to 200°C and the time to 15 minutes. Press the START/STOP button to begin cooking.
6. After 7 minutes of cooking, open the air fryer and flip the corn cobs to ensure even cooking.
7. Close the air fryer and continue cooking for the remaining 8 minutes, or until the corn kernels are tender and slightly charred.
8. Once the cooking is complete, remove the corn cobs from Zone 1.
9. Garnish with fresh parsley.
10. Serve the **Corn on the Cob** warm as a delicious and classic side dish, perfect for summer BBQs or any meal.

CHAPTER 08: VEGETARIAN

Crispy Onion Rings

Prep: 15 Min | Cook: 15 Min | Serves: 4

Ingredient:

- 2 large onions
- 100g plain flour
- 1 teaspoon garlic powder
- 1/2 teaspoon paprika
- 1/2 teaspoon salt
- 1/4 teaspoon black pepper
- 200ml plant-based milk (such as almond or soy milk)
- 100g bread crumbs
- Cooking spray or oil, for greasing

Instruction:

1. Peel the onions and cut them into 1 cm thick slices. Separate the slices into individual rings.
2. In a shallow bowl, combine the plain flour, garlic powder, paprika, salt, and black pepper.
3. Pour the plant-based milk into another shallow bowl. Dip each onion ring into the flour mixture, ensuring it is fully coated. Shake off any excess flour.
4. Dip the floured onion ring into the plant-based milk, allowing any excess milk to drip off.
5. Roll the onion ring in the bread crumbs, pressing lightly to adhere the coating.
6. Grease Zone 1 of the air fryer basket with cooking spray or oil. Place the breaded onion rings in Zone 1 of the air fryer basket.
7. Select Zone 1 and the AIR FRY program. Set the temperature to 200°C for 15 minutes. Press the START/STOP.
8. After 7 minutes of cooking, open the air fryer and flip the onion rings for even browning. Close the air fryer and continue cooking for the remaining 8 minutes, or until the onion rings are crispy and golden brown.
9. Once the cooking is complete, remove the onion rings from Zone 1.
10. Serve the **Crispy Onion Rings** immediately as a tasty appetizer or side dish, perfect for dipping in vegan-friendly sauces.

Crispy Polenta Fries

Prep: 10 Min | Cook: 20 Min | Serves: 4

Ingredient:

- 250g instant polenta
- 1 litre vegetable stock
- 1 teaspoon garlic powder
- 1 teaspoon paprika
- 1/2 teaspoon salt
- 1/4 teaspoon black pepper
- Cooking spray or oil, for greasing

Instruction:

1. In a large saucepan, bring the vegetable stock to a boil. Gradually whisk in the instant polenta, garlic powder, paprika, salt, and black pepper.
2. Continue whisking for about 5 minutes, or until the polenta thickens and pulls away from the sides of the pan.
3. Pour the cooked polenta onto a greased baking tray, spreading it evenly to a thickness of about 2 cm. Allow it to cool and set for about 10 minutes.
4. Once the polenta has cooled and set, cut it into long fries, approximately 1 cm wide.
5. Grease Zone 1 of the air fryer basket with cooking spray or oil.
6. Place the polenta fries in Zone 1 of the air fryer basket, making sure they are in a single layer.
7. Select Zone 1 and the AIR FRY program. Set the temperature to 200°C and the time to 20 minutes. Press the START/STOP button to begin cooking.
8. After 10 minutes of cooking, open the air fryer and flip the polenta fries for even browning.
9. Close the air fryer and continue cooking for the remaining 10 minutes, or until the polenta fries are crispy and golden brown.
10. Serve the **Crispy Polenta Fries** immediately as a delicious and unique side dish or snack.

CHAPTER 08: VEGETARIAN

Crispy Tofu

Prep: 15 Min | Cook: 20 Min | Serves: 4

Ingredient:

- 400g firm tofu
- 2 tablespoons cornstarch
- 1 teaspoon garlic powder
- 1/2 teaspoon paprika
- 1/2 teaspoon salt
- 1/4 teaspoon black pepper
- Cooking spray or oil, for greasing

Instruction:

1. Drain the tofu and wrap it in a clean kitchen towel or paper towels. Place a heavy object, such as a plate or a book, on top of the wrapped tofu and let it sit for about 10 minutes to remove excess moisture.
2. Cut the tofu into bite-sized cubes or rectangles.
3. In a shallow bowl, combine the cornstarch, garlic powder, paprika, salt, and black pepper.
4. Toss the tofu cubes in the cornstarch mixture until they are evenly coated.
5. Grease Zone 1 of the air fryer basket with cooking spray or oil.
6. Place the coated tofu cubes in Zone 1 of the air fryer basket, making sure they are in a single layer.
7. Select Zone 1 and the AIR FRY program. Set the temperature to 200°C and the time to 20 minutes. Press the START/STOP button to begin cooking.
8. After 10 minutes of cooking, open the air fryer and shake the basket to flip the tofu cubes for even browning.
9. Close the air fryer and continue cooking for the remaining 10 minutes, or until the tofu cubes are crispy and golden brown.
10. Serve the **Crispy Tofu** immediately as a protein-packed main dish or as a tasty addition to salads, stir-fries, or rice bowls.

Falafel

Prep: 15 Min | Cook: 15 Min | Serves: 20 falafel

Ingredient:

- 250g dried chickpeas
- 1 small onion, roughly chopped
- 2 garlic cloves
- 1 small bunch fresh parsley
- 1 small bunch fresh cilantro (coriander)
- 1 teaspoon ground cumin
- 1 teaspoon ground coriander
- 1/2 teaspoon baking powder
- 1 tablespoon plain flour
- 1 tablespoon lemon juice
- 1/2 teaspoon salt
- Cooking spray or oil, for greasing

Instruction:

1. Place the dried chickpeas in a large bowl and cover them with cold water. Let them soak overnight or for at least 8 hours. Drain and rinse the chickpeas before using.
2. In a food processor, combine the soaked chickpeas, onion, garlic cloves, fresh parsley, fresh cilantro, ground cumin, ground coriander, baking powder, plain flour, lemon juice, and salt. Process until the mixture forms a coarse paste.
3. Shape the falafel mixture into small balls or patties, approximately 3 cm in diameter, and place them in Zone 1 and Zone 2 of the air fryer basket. Ensure they are in a single layer and not overcrowded.
4. Select Zone 1 and the AIR FRY program. Set the temperature to 200°C for 15 minutes. Select MATCH. Press the START/STOP.
5. After 8 minutes of cooking, open the air fryer and flip the falafel for even browning.
6. Close the air fryer and continue cooking for the remaining 7 minutes, or until the falafel is crispy and golden brown.
7. Serve the **Falafel** immediately as a delicious and protein-rich main dish or as a filling for wraps or sandwiches. They are traditionally served with hummus, tahini sauce, or a fresh salad.

CHAPTER 08: VEGETARIAN

Garlic Mushrooms

Prep: 10 Min | Cook: 10 Min | Serves: 4

Ingredient:

- 500g button mushrooms, cleaned and halved
- 3 tablespoons olive oil
- 4 cloves garlic, minced
- 1 tablespoon fresh thyme leaves
- 1/2 teaspoon salt
- 1/4 teaspoon black pepper
- Cooking spray or oil, for greasing

Instruction:

1. In a bowl, combine the olive oil, minced garlic, fresh thyme leaves, salt, and black pepper.
2. Add the halved mushrooms to the bowl and toss them in the oil and garlic mixture until they are well coated.
3. Grease Zone 1 of the air fryer basket with cooking spray or oil.
4. Place the coated mushrooms in Zone 1 of the air fryer basket, making sure they are in a single layer.
5. Select Zone 1 and the AIR FRY program. Set the temperature to 200°C and the time to 10 minutes. Press the START/STOP button to begin cooking.
6. After 5 minutes of cooking, open the air fryer and shake the basket to toss the mushrooms for even cooking.
7. Close the air fryer and continue cooking for the remaining 5 minutes, or until the mushrooms are tender and lightly browned.
8. Once the cooking is complete, remove the garlic mushrooms from Zone 1.
9. Serve the **Garlic Mushrooms** immediately as a flavorful side dish or as a topping for toast, pasta, or rice.

Halloumi Fries

Prep: 15 Min | Cook: 15 Min | Serves: 4

Ingredient:

- 250g firm tofu
- 2 tablespoons cornstarch
- 2 tablespoons nutritional yeast
- 1 tablespoon lemon juice
- 1/2 teaspoon garlic powder
- 1/2 teaspoon dried oregano
- 1/2 teaspoon salt
- Cooking spray or oil, for greasing

Instruction:

1. Drain the tofu and wrap it in a clean kitchen towel or paper towels. Place a heavy object, such as a plate or a book, on top of the wrapped tofu and let it sit for about 10 minutes to remove excess moisture.
2. Cut the tofu into long, thin fries, approximately 1 cm wide.
3. In a shallow bowl, combine the cornstarch, nutritional yeast, lemon juice, garlic powder, dried oregano, and salt. Toss the tofu fries in the cornstarch mixture until they are evenly coated.
4. Grease Zone 1 of the air fryer basket with cooking spray or oil.
5. Place the coated tofu fries in Zone 1 of the air fryer basket.
6. Select Zone 1 and the AIR FRY program. Set the temperature to 200°C and the time to 15 minutes. Press the START/STOP button to begin cooking.
7. After 8 minutes of cooking, open the air fryer and shake the basket to flip the tofu fries for even browning.
8. Close the air fryer and continue cooking for the remaining 7 minutes, or until the tofu fries are crispy and lightly golden.
9. Serve the **Halloumi Fries** immediately as a delicious and vegan-friendly alternative to traditional Halloumi fries. They can be enjoyed on their own or served with your favorite dipping sauce.

CHAPTER 08: VEGETARIAN

Mushroom Wellington

Prep: 30 Min | Cook: 25 Min | Serves: 4

Ingredient:

- 500g mixed mushrooms (such as button, cremini, or portobello), finely chopped
- 1 onion, finely chopped
- 2 garlic cloves, minced
- 2 tablespoons olive oil
- 1 tablespoon soy sauce
- 1 tablespoon balsamic vinegar
- 1 teaspoon dried thyme
- Salt and pepper, to taste
- 320g vegan puff pastry, thawed if frozen
- 1 tablespoon plant-based milk, for brushing

Instruction:

1. In a large pan, heat the olive oil over medium heat. Add the chopped onions and minced garlic, and sauté until softened and slightly golden, about 5 minutes.
2. Add the finely chopped mushrooms, soy sauce, balsamic vinegar, dried thyme, salt, and pepper to the pan. Cook, stirring occasionally, until the mushrooms have released their moisture and it has evaporated, about 10 minutes. Remove from heat and let the mixture cool.
3. Roll out the vegan puff pastry on a lightly floured surface to a rectangle approximately 30cm x 25cm. Spread the cooled mushroom mixture evenly over the puff pastry.
4. Carefully roll up the puff pastry, starting from one long side, until you have a log shape. Seal the edges by pressing them gently.
5. Transfer the mushroom Wellington to Zone 1 of the air fryer basket, seam side down.
6. Select Zone 1 and the AIR FRY program. Set the temperature to 200°C for 25 minutes. Press the START/STOP.
7. After 20 minutes of cooking, open the air fryer and brush the top of the Wellington with plant-based milk for a golden finish.
8. Close the air fryer and continue cooking for the remaining 5 minutes, or until the puff pastry is crisp and golden.
9. Let the Wellington rest for a few minutes before slicing into thick portions. Serve the **Mushroom Wellington** as a delightful centerpiece for a special occasion or a comforting main dish.

Stuffed Bell Peppers

Prep: 20 Min | Cook: 25 Min | Serves: 4

Ingredient:

- 4 large bell peppers
- 200g cooked quinoa
- 1 onion, finely chopped
- 2 cloves garlic, minced
- 1 carrot, grated
- 1 zucchini, grated
- 200g canned diced tomatoes
- 100g canned sweetcorn
- 1 teaspoon dried oregano
- 1 teaspoon ground cumin
- Salt and pepper, to taste
- Cooking spray or oil, for greasing

Instruction:

1. Cut the tops off the bell peppers and remove the seeds and membranes. Set aside.
2. In a large pan, heat some cooking spray or oil over medium heat. Add the chopped onions and minced garlic, and sauté until softened and slightly golden, about 5 minutes. Add the grated carrot and zucchini to the pan and cook for an additional 3 minutes, until slightly softened.
3. Stir in the cooked quinoa, diced tomatoes, sweetcorn, dried oregano, ground cumin, salt, and pepper. Cook for another 5 minutes to allow the flavors to meld together.
4. Stuff the bell peppers with the quinoa and vegetable mixture, pressing it down gently. Place the stuffed bell peppers in Zone 1 of the air fryer basket.
5. Select Zone 1 and the AIR FRY program. Set the temperature to 180°C for 25 minutes. Press the START/STOP.
6. After 15 minutes of cooking, open the air fryer and rotate the bell peppers for even cooking.
7. Close the air fryer and continue cooking for the remaining 10 minutes, or until the bell peppers are tender and slightly charred.
8. Let the bell peppers cool for a few minutes before serving.
9. Serve the **Stuffed Bell Peppers** as a nutritious and satisfying main course.

CHAPTER 08: VEGETARIAN

Stuffed Mushrooms

Prep: 15 Min | Cook: 15 Min | Serves: 12 stuffed

Ingredient:

- 12 large button mushrooms
- 1 tablespoon olive oil
- 1 onion, finely chopped
- 2 cloves garlic, minced
- 100g breadcrumbs
- 50g vegan cream cheese
- 2 tablespoons nutritional yeast
- 1 tablespoon fresh parsley, chopped
- Salt and pepper, to taste
- Cooking spray or oil, for greasing

Instruction:

1. Remove the stems from the button mushrooms and set them aside. Clean the mushroom caps with a damp cloth or paper towel. Finely chop the mushroom stems.
2. In a large pan, heat the olive oil over medium heat. Add the chopped onion and minced garlic, and sauté until softened and slightly golden, about 5 minutes.
3. Add the chopped mushroom stems to the pan and cook for an additional 3 minutes, until they release their moisture and become tender.
4. In a bowl, combine the cooked mushroom stem mixture, breadcrumbs, vegan cream cheese, nutritional yeast, chopped parsley, salt, and pepper. Mix well.
5. Spoon the stuffing mixture into each mushroom cap, filling them generously. Place the stuffed mushrooms in both zones of the air fryer basket.
6. Select Zone 1 and the AIR FRY program. Set the temperature to 180°C for 15 minutes. Select MATCH. Press the START/STOP.
7. After 8 minutes of cooking, open the air fryer and shake the basket to ensure even cooking. Close the air fryer and continue cooking for the remaining 7 minutes.
8. Let the mushrooms cool for a few minutes before serving.
9. Serve the **Stuffed Mushrooms** as an appetizer or party snack. They can be enjoyed hot or at room temperature.

Stuffed Tomatoes

Prep: 15 Min | Cook: 15 Min | Serves: 4

Ingredient:

- 4 large tomatoes
- 100g breadcrumbs
- 1 small onion, finely chopped
- 2 cloves garlic, minced
- 100g grated cheddar or vegan cheese
- 2 tablespoons fresh parsley, chopped
- 2 tablespoons olive oil
- Salt and pepper, to taste
- Cooking spray or oil, for greasing

▶ Instruction:

1. Cut off the top of each tomato and scoop out the seeds and pulp, creating hollow tomato cups. Set the tomato cups aside.
2. In a bowl, combine the breadcrumbs, finely chopped onion, minced garlic, grated cheddar or vegan cheese, chopped parsley, olive oil, salt, and pepper. Mix well until all the ingredients are evenly incorporated.
3. Stuff each tomato cup with the breadcrumb mixture, pressing it down gently. Make sure to fill the tomatoes without overflowing.
4. Place the stuffed tomatoes in Zone 1 of the air fryer basket.
5. Select Zone 1 and the AIR FRY program. Set the temperature to 180°C and the time to 15 minutes. Press the START/STOP button to begin cooking.
6. After 8 minutes of cooking, open the air fryer and check the doneness of the tomatoes. If they are not yet tender, close the air fryer and continue cooking for the remaining time.
7. Let the tomatoes cool for a few minutes before serving.
8. Serve the **Stuffed Tomatoes** as a delightful side dish or a light vegetarian main course. They can be enjoyed hot or at room temperature.

CHAPTER 08: VEGETARIAN

Sweet Potato Hash Browns

Prep: 15 Min | Cook: 20 Min | Serves: 4

Ingredient:

- 500g sweet potatoes, peeled and grated
- 1 small onion, finely chopped
- 2 tablespoons cornflour
- 1 teaspoon smoked paprika
- 1/2 teaspoon garlic powder
- Salt and pepper, to taste
- Cooking spray or oil, for greasing

▶ Instruction:

1. Place the grated sweet potatoes in a clean kitchen towel or cheesecloth. Squeeze out any excess moisture from the sweet potatoes.
2. In a large bowl, combine the grated sweet potatoes, finely chopped onion, cornflour, smoked paprika, garlic powder, salt, and pepper. Mix well.
3. Grease Zone 1 of the air fryer basket with cooking spray or oil.
4. Take a portion of the sweet potato mixture and shape it into a round, flat hash brown. Repeat with the remaining mixture to make 8 hash browns in total. Place the hash browns in Zone 1 of the air fryer basket.
5. Select Zone 1 and the AIR FRY program. Set the temperature to 200°C for 20 minutes. Press the START/STOP.
6. After 10 minutes of cooking, open the air fryer and flip the hash browns to ensure even browning.
7. Close the air fryer and continue cooking for the remaining 10 minutes, or until the hash browns are crispy and golden brown.
8. Let the hash browns cool for a few minutes before serving.
9. Serve the **Sweet Potato Hash Browns** as a delicious breakfast or brunch option. They can be enjoyed on their own or served with your favorite vegan sauce or condiments.

Vegetable Kebabs

Prep: 20 Min | Cook: 15 Min | Serves: 4

Ingredient:

- 1 red bell pepper, cut into chunks
- 1 green bell pepper, cut into chunks
- 1 yellow bell pepper, cut into chunks
- 1 red onion, cut into chunks
- 200g button mushrooms
- 200g cherry tomatoes
- 2 tablespoons olive oil
- 1 tablespoon balsamic vinegar
- 1 teaspoon dried mixed herbs
- Salt and pepper, to taste
- Wooden or metal skewers
- Cooking spray or oil, for greasing

➤ Instruction:

1. In a large bowl, combine the olive oil, balsamic vinegar, dried mixed herbs, salt, and pepper. Mix well to create a marinade.
2. Add the bell peppers, red onion, mushrooms, and cherry tomatoes to the bowl with the marinade. Toss the vegetables until they are evenly coated.
3. Thread the marinated vegetables onto skewers, alternating the different vegetables. Leave some space between each piece to ensure even cooking.
4. Grease Zone 1 of the air fryer basket with cooking spray or oil.
5. Place the vegetable kebabs in Zone 1 of the air fryer basket.
6. Select Zone 1 and the AIR FRY program. Set the temperature to 200°C and the time to 15 minutes. Press the START/STOP button to begin cooking.
7. After 8 minutes of cooking, open the air fryer and carefully flip the kebabs to ensure even browning.
8. Close the air fryer and continue cooking for the remaining 7 minutes or until the vegetables are tender and slightly charred.
9. Once the cooking is complete, remove the Vegetable Kebabs from Zone 1. Let the kebabs cool for a few minutes before serving.
10. Serve the **Vegetable Kebabs** as a delicious main course or as a side dish with a dip of your choice.

CHAPTER 08: VEGETARIAN

Vegetable Tempura

Prep: 20 Min | Cook: 10 Min | Serves: 4

Ingredient:

For the Tempura Batter:
- 100g plain flour
- 2 tablespoons cornflour
- 1/2 teaspoon baking powder
- 1/2 teaspoon salt
- 240ml ice-cold sparkling water

For the Vegetable Tempura:
- 1 small courgette, cut into thin slices
- 1 small aubergine, cut into thin slices
- 1 red bell pepper, cut into strips
- 1 green bell pepper, cut into strips
- 1 small onion, thinly sliced
- Vegetable oil, for greasing
- Soy sauce or dipping sauce, for serving (optional)

➤ Instruction:

1. In a large bowl, whisk together the plain flour, cornflour, baking powder, and salt to make the tempura batter.
2. Gradually pour in the ice-cold sparkling water while whisking the batter until it becomes smooth and free of lumps. The batter should have a thin consistency.
3. Grease both zone of the air fryer basket with vegetable oil.
4. Dip the vegetable slices into the tempura batter, ensuring they are evenly coated.
5. Evenly dividing battered vegetables between the two zone, leaving some space between each piece.
6. Select Zone 1 and the AIR FRY program. Set the temperature to 200°C and the time to 10 minutes. Select MATCH to duplicate settings across both zones. Press the START/STOP button to begin cooking.
7. After 5 minutes of cooking, open the air fryer and carefully flip the vegetable tempura to ensure even browning.
8. Close the air fryer and continue cooking for the remaining 5 minutes or until the tempura is crispy and golden brown.
9. Once the cooking is complete, remove the Vegetable Tempura from Zone 1. Let the tempura cool for a few minutes before serving.
10. Serve the **Vegetable Tempura** as an appetizer or a side dish. It can be enjoyed on its own or served with soy sauce or a dipping sauce of your choice.

Vegetarian Meatballs

Prep: 30 Min | Cook: 15 Min

Serves: 20 meatballs

Ingredient:

- 200g cooked lentils
- 200g cooked chickpeas
- 1 small onion, finely chopped
- 2 cloves garlic, minced
- 2 tablespoons tomato paste
- 2 tablespoons nutritional yeast
- 2 tablespoons soy sauce
- 1 teaspoon dried mixed herbs
- 1/2 teaspoon paprika
- 50g breadcrumbs
- Salt and pepper, to taste
- Cooking spray or oil, for greasing

Instruction:

1. In a large bowl, combine the cooked lentils, cooked chickpeas, finely chopped onion, minced garlic, tomato paste, nutritional yeast, soy sauce, dried mixed herbs, paprika, breadcrumbs, salt, and pepper.
2. Use a potato masher or fork to mash the ingredients together until well combined. The mixture should hold together when pressed. Shape the mixture into small meatball-sized balls, approximately 3cm in diameter.
3. Place the vegetarian meatballs in both zones of the air fryer basket, leaving space between each one.
4. Select Zone 1 and the AIR FRY program. Set the temperature to 200°C for 15 minutes. Select MATCH. Press the START/STOP.
5. After 8 minutes of cooking, open the air fryer and carefully flip the meatballs to ensure even browning. Close the air fryer and continue cooking for the remaining 7 minutes or until the meatballs are crispy on the outside and heated through.
6. Once the cooking is complete, remove the Vegetarian Meatballs from Zone 1. Let the meatballs cool for a few minutes before serving.
7. Serve the **Vegetarian Meatballs** as a main course or as a delicious addition to pasta, salads, or sandwiches.

CHAPTER 08: VEGETARIAN

Vegetarian Quesadillas

Prep: 15 Min | Cook: 10 Min

Serves: 4 quesadillas

Ingredient:

- 4 large flour tortillas
- 200g vegan cheese, grated (such as vegan cheddar or mozzarella)
- 1 small red onion, thinly sliced
- 1 small red bell pepper, thinly sliced
- 1 small green bell pepper, thinly sliced
- 1 small courgette, thinly sliced
- 1 teaspoon olive oil
- Salt and pepper, to taste
- Cooking spray or oil, for greasing

Instruction:

1. In a frying pan, heat the olive oil over medium heat. Add the sliced red onion, red bell pepper, green bell pepper, and courgette. Sauté the vegetables for about 5 minutes until they are slightly softened. Season with salt and pepper to taste. Remove from heat.
2. Sprinkle approximately 50g of the grated vegan cheese evenly over half of the tortilla. Add a portion of the sautéed vegetables on top of the cheese.
3. Fold the tortilla in half to cover the filling and press down gently.
4. Evenly dividing quesadillas between the two zone, leaving space between each one.
5. Select Zone 1 and the AIR FRY program. Set the temperature to 200°C and the time to 10 minutes. Select MATCH to duplicate settings across both zones. Press the START/STOP button to begin cooking.
6. After 5 minutes of cooking, open the air fryer and carefully flip the quesadillas to ensure even browning. Close the air fryer and continue cooking for the remaining 5 minutes or until the quesadillas are crispy and the vegan cheese is melted.
7. Let the quesadillas cool for a few minutes before serving.
8. Cut each **Vegetarian Quesadillas** into wedges and serve hot. You can serve them with salsa, guacamole, or vegan sour cream as dipping sauces, if desired.

Printed in Great Britain
by Amazon